# Weeknight
# DESSERTS

D1114546

# Weeknight
# DESSERTS
## Quick & Easy
## Sweet Treats

### BEATRICE OJAKANGAS

SELLERS
PUBLISHING

Published by Sellers Publishing, Inc.

Text copyright © 2010 Beatrice Ojakangas
All rights reserved.
Author photo (back flap) copyright Brett Groehler.

Sellers Publishing, Inc.
161 John Roberts Road, South Portland, Maine 04106
For ordering information:
(800) 625-3386 toll free
Visit our Web site: www.sellerspublishing.com • E-mail: rsp@rsvp.com

ISBN: 13: 978-1-4162-0590-6

Library of Congress Control Number: 2010924371

10 9 8 7 6 5 4 3 2 1

Printed and bound in China.

## Dedication

*To all those dessert lovers out there who think there just isn't time — but there really is!*

# CONTENTS

## INTRODUCTION

There is always time for dessert. For some, dinner isn't dinner without a dessert. For others, dessert is simply a welcome treat. A sweet ending to a meal may be one way to transform an otherwise light meal into something satisfying.

Whether you need to whip up something at the last minute, or make something ahead of time, this collection of dessert recipes is designed to help you out of a "what's for dessert?" dilemma. Some easy classics need to be made ahead so that they can set. These are candidates for tomorrow night's dessert. Others might require some minutes of baking or just a few minutes of chilling. They are candidates for tonight's desserts.

We focus on desserts that you can serve any night of the week, but "any night" does not need to be "everyday." When time and energy are short, ice cream and fresh fruit can step in to make splendid desserts. Desserts can add to the overall nutritional value of a meal. Or, they can be the bite of delight that excites. You will find both options in this collection of desserts.

Except for fresh fruits that are in season, most of the ingredients are standard staples found in a well-stocked kitchen. Because we're talking efficiency here, be sure to read through the recipe and collect the ingredients and utensils needed. It's also a good idea to keep a running tab of the staples and replenish them before you run out. There is nothing more frustrating than to find you need a cup of sugar and you only have a half cup in stock, or that you need three eggs and there are only two in the refrigerator.

# How to use this book

You will notice icons used throughout the book to help you identify special features of the recipes at a glance.

indicates that you'll find a handy tip or explanation that relates to that recipe.

highlights some distinct flavor and ingredient variations you can make to alter the main recipe on that page. The changes to ingredients are simple, but the end results are a whole new delightful treat.

alerts you to the amazing simplicity of the recipe. Any recipe with this icon tells you that all the prep work for the recipe can be completed in a single bowl or pan. Fewer dirty dishes are always a bonus when you're in a hurry.

signals a recipe that can or must be prepared ahead. While all these recipes are quick to come together, some need time in the refrigerator or freezer. Other recipes with this icon simply offer make-ahead instructions for those predictably time-crunched evenings.

# One Batch Cookies & Bars

Mix them while the oven preheats and bake in a single pan

- Chocolate Fudge Oatmeal Cookies

- Peanut Butter Cornflake Crunch Squares

- Chocolate Berry Crumble Bars

- Butterscotch Pecan Refrigerator Cookies

- Basic Butter Slice-and-Bake Cookies

- English Toffee Bars

- Honey Maple Pecan Diamonds

- Shortbread

- Brown Sugar Shortbread

- Chocolate Chip Platter Cookies

- Double Chocolate Chunk Platter Cookies

- One-Bowl Cocoa Bars

- Saucepan Brownies

- Walnut Butterscotch Blondies

- Applesauce Bars

- Flourless Quick Peanut Butter Cookies

- Irish Oatmeal Brownies

- Raspberry Butter Cookie Strips

# Chocolate Fudge Oatmeal Cookies

*When time is short and you need cookies in a hurry, you can make these cookies with ingredients commonly found on the cupboard shelf. If you open a fresh can of evaporated milk, you can use the remainder in a creamy soup, use it as liquid in a bread or cake, or freeze it up to a month, ideally in ice cube trays. When frozen, turn the cubes into a freezer bag and use as needed.*

1 cup sugar
¼ cup evaporated milk
2 tablespoons unsweetened cocoa powder
1 ounce (¼ stick) butter
1 teaspoon vanilla extract
½ cup chopped walnuts or pecans
1¼ cups quick-cooking oats

In a medium saucepan, combine the sugar, milk, cocoa, and butter. Bring to a boil over medium heat, stirring constantly; boil for 1 minute. Remove from heat; stir in vanilla and nuts. Add oatmeal and stir in to blend well. Drop by teaspoonfuls onto waxed paper. Cookies are ready to eat when cool and dry to the touch.

You can make these no-bake cookies in 5 minutes or less. To reduce the fat and sugar you can use low-fat evaporated milk and replace half the sugar with a sugar substitute.

**Makes:** about 2 dozen cookies

# Peanut Butter Corn Flake Crunch Squares

*With just four ingredients you can quickly put together these squares.*

. . . . . . . . . . . . . . . . . . . . . . . . . . . . . . . . . . . . . . . . . . . . . . . . . . . . . . . . . . . . . . . . . . . . . . . . . . .

1 cup sugar

½ cup dark corn syrup

1 cup peanut butter

5 cups corn flakes

. . . . . . . . . . . . . . . . . . . . . . . . . . . . . . . . . . . . . . . . . . . . . . . . . . . . . . . . . . . . . . . . . . . . . . . . . . .

In a saucepan, combine the sugar and syrup; bring to a boil, stirring constantly. Remove from the heat. Add the peanut butter and corn flakes. Mix well. Spread mixture into a 9-inch square pan and press firmly into an even layer. Cool. Cut into 18 squares.

. . . . . . . . . . . . . . . . . . . . . . . . . . . . . . . . . . . . . . . . . . . . . . . . . . . . . . . . . . . . . . . . . . . . . . . . . . .

This is a no-bake recipe. To turn these no-bake bars into cookies, drop rounded spoonfuls of the warm mixture onto waxed paper and allow to cool. Store in an airtight container in a cool place. Separate layers of the cookies or squares with waxed paper.

**Makes:** 18 squares

. . . . . . . . . . . . . . . . . . . . . . . . . . . . . . . . . . . . . . . . . . . . . . . . . . . . . . . . . . . . . . . . . . . . . . . . . . .

# Chocolate Berry Crumble Bars

*Fruit fillings between nutty, rich crusts were the beginning of a number of bar cookies so popular today.*

8 ounces (2 sticks) butter, softened

1 cup packed light brown sugar

1½ cups all-purpose flour

½ teaspoon salt

1½ cups uncooked rolled oats, old-fashioned or quick

½ cup sweetened flaked coconut

½ cup chopped walnuts or pecans

¾ cup semisweet chocolate chips

2 cups strawberry or raspberry preserves

Preheat the oven to 350°F. Butter and flour a 13x9-inch baking dish.

In a large bowl, cream the butter and brown sugar. In a separate bowl, mix the flour, and salt together and blend into the creamed mixture. Add the rolled oats, coconut, and nuts and mix until crumbly. Press half of the crumb mixture into the buttered pan and flatten with hands to cover the bottom of the pan. Sprinkle with the chocolate chips. Spread the preserves over evenly. Cover with remaining crumb mixture. Pat lightly to compress the layers. Bake for 25 to 30 minutes until lightly browned. Cut into bars while still warm.

To make **Luscious Date Bars,** cook 3 cups cut-up pitted dates with ¼ cup sugar in 1½ cups water over low heat until thickened, about 10 minutes. Cool and use in place of the preserves.

For people with nut allergies, these are just as delicious if you leave out the walnuts or pecans.

**Makes:** 32 bars

# Butterscotch Pecan Refrigerator Cookies

*This makes a large amount of cookies, but the idea here is to shape the dough into rolls and store the extra dough in the refrigerator or freezer. Slice and bake when you need cookies in a hurry. You can keep the rolls in the refrigerator up to one week, or in the freezer up to two months, well wrapped.*

6 ounces (1½ sticks) butter
1 cup packed light brown sugar
1 teaspoon vanilla extract
1 large egg, beaten
1½ cups all-purpose flour
1½ teaspoons baking powder
¼ teaspoon salt
½ cup chopped pecans

In a mixing bowl, using a hand mixer, cream the butter with the sugar until smooth. Increase the speed to high and beat in the vanilla and egg. In a separate bowl, stir the flour, baking powder, salt and pecans together. Stir into the creamed mixture until well blended. On a clean work surface, shape dough into a roll about 2 inches in diameter. Wrap in waxed paper, plastic wrap, or foil. Refrigerate until thoroughly chilled.

**To bake:** Preheat oven to 350°F. Cut the roll into ⅛-inch-thick slices and arrange on an ungreased baking sheet (refrigerate remaining dough). Bake for 8 to 10 minutes until lightly browned.

To prevent the unbaked dough from picking up flavors and odors from the refrigerator or freezer, wrap tightly first in waxed paper or plastic wrap, then in foil. Eliminate the pecans for people with nut allergies.

To make **Pecan Chocolate Refrigerator Cookies,** use granulated sugar instead of the brown sugar and add 2 squares of melted unsweetened chocolate to the butter and sugar mixture.

**Makes:** 6 dozen cookies

# Basic Butter Slice-and-Bake Cookies

*Keep a log of this cookie dough in the refrigerator or freezer so that you can quickly bake a batch whenever the craving or need strikes. You can keep the dough in the refrigerator up to one week, or in the freezer up to two months, well wrapped.*

8 ounces (2 sticks) butter, softened

½ cup granulated sugar

½ cup packed light or dark brown sugar

2 large eggs

2¾ cups all-purpose flour

½ teaspoon baking soda

⅛ teaspoon salt

In a large bowl, cream the butter with the granulated and brown sugars. Beat in the eggs. In a separate bowl, mix the flour, baking soda, and salt. Stir into the creamed mixture until well blended. Divide the dough into three parts and shape each into a log. Wrap each log in plastic wrap or waxed paper. Chill. If desired, wrap the logs in foil and freeze until later.

**To bake:** Preheat the oven to 350°F. Cover a baking sheet with parchment paper. Slice dough into ¼-inch-thick rounds and place on the parchment-covered sheet, about 2 inches apart. Bake for 12 minutes.

For **Fruited Cookies** or **Fruit and Nut Cookies** add ½ cup dried fruit (dark or golden raisins, dried cranberries, or chopped dates) and ½ cup chopped nuts (pecans or walnuts) — for a total addition of 1 cup fruit and/or nut combination — to the creamed mixture.

For **Chocolate Cookies,** blend 2 squares of melted unsweetened chocolate into the creamed mixture.

For **Orange-Almond Cookies,** stir 1 tablespoon grated orange zest into the creamed mixture and add ½ cup toasted, chopped blanched almonds to the dough along with the flour mixture.

**Makes:** 6 dozen 2½ inch cookies

# English Toffee Bars

*Even the most die-hard brownie lovers seem to fall for this one. Crispy and buttery, these squares require little effort to mix up. The secret to their success is a full hour of baking at a low temperature. So, once you get them into the oven, set the timer and go about your business until these delights are ready.*

8 ounces (2 sticks) butter, softened
1 cup packed dark brown sugar
1 large egg, separated
2 cups all-purpose flour
1 cup slivered or sliced almonds

Preheat the oven to 275°F. Coat a 15x10-inch rimmed baking sheet with cooking spray. In the large bowl of an electric mixer, beat the butter and sugar until creamy. Add the egg yolk (reserve the white) and mix. Blend the flour into the creamed mixture to make a stiff cookie dough. Press the dough evenly over the bottom of the baking pan. Beat the egg white lightly and then brush it over the dough to cover evenly. Sprinkle the almonds over the top and press in lightly.

Bake for 1 hour or until firm when lightly touched. While still hot, cut into 1½-inch squares. Let cool in the pan on a rack.

 Replace the sliced almonds with chopped pecans or walnuts.

 For **Chocolate-Frosted English Toffee Bars**, omit the nuts and sprinkle 1 cup semisweet chocolate chips over the hot bars. Heat from the bars will melt the chocolate. Spread melted chocolate over the bars evenly.

**Makes:** 6 dozen bars

# Honey Maple Pecan Diamonds

*If you are a lover of pecan pie, one of these little diamond-shaped bites may be all you need to be satisfied. The easy press-in crust speeds the preparation process.*

12 ounces (3 sticks) chilled butter, divided

1½ cups all-purpose flour

¼ cup ice water

1½ cups packed light brown sugar

¼ cup maple syrup

¼ cup honey

½ cup granulated sugar

4 cups chopped pecans

¼ cup heavy whipping cream

Preheat the oven to 375°F. Coat a 13x9-inch baking pan with cooking spray and dust with flour. In a large mixing bowl or in a food processor, cut 4 ounces (1 stick) of the butter into the flour until crumbly. Add the water and use a fork to combine until moist crumbs form. Turn crumbs into the baking pan and press evenly over the bottom and about 1 inch up the sides of the pan.

In a saucepan, melt the remaining 8 ounces (2 sticks) of butter and add the brown sugar, maple syrup, honey, and granulated sugar. Bring to a boil, stirring constantly. Boil 4 minutes until thickened. Remove from heat and stir in the pecans and cream. Pour evenly into the crumb-lined pan. Bake for 25 minutes or until the edges are browned. Cool in the pan. Cut into 1-inch strips, then cut diagonally into 1-inch pieces to create the diamond shapes.

These bar cookies keep well when packed in an airtight container and frozen. Separate the layers with waxed paper.

**Makes:** about 50 diamond-shaped bars

# Shortbread

*True shortbread is the most basic of all cookie recipes. Butter, flour, and sugar are the major ingredients. If the butter is salted, you don't even add salt. True shortbread has a melt-in-your-mouth texture that is crisp, yet crumbly. The classic ingredient ratio is 3 parts flour, 2 parts butter, and 1 part sugar, which makes a very rich shortbread. This recipe is slightly less rich, but still has a delicious buttery flavor.*

1½ cups all-purpose flour
4 ounces (1 stick) butter, softened
¼ cup sugar

Preheat the oven to 325°F. Cover a baking sheet with parchment paper. Combine the flour, butter, and sugar in the work bowl of a food processor with the steel blade in place. Process until the dough has the consistency of a short crust. Alternatively, combine the ingredients in a large mixing bowl and mix with a hand mixer until a smooth dough forms. Form the dough into a ball and press the dough evenly onto the prepared baking sheet to make a 7-inch round. Score into 8 to 12 wedges with a straight-edged knife, but leave the wedges in place. Use a fork to make impressions around the edge of the dough; then pierce each wedge 3 times. Bake for 35 to 40 minutes until pale golden brown. Remove from the oven and, while still warm, cut along the scored lines. Cool the shortbread, leaving the wedges in place. Once cooled and firm, transfer shortbread to a plate to serve or to a container to store. Shortbread can be stored at room temperature in a cool, dark place, or frozen for up to 3 months.

To make **Cinnamon Shortbread,** add 1 teaspoon ground cinnamon to the dough.

For **Oat Shortbread** (good for people with wheat allergies): Replace the flour with oat flour. To make oat flour, put dry uncooked rolled oats into blender; process on high to make 1½ cups oat flour. Continue with regular Shortbread baking instructions, but skip the scoring. (Oat Shortbread bakes together and scored lines will not be visible.)

**Shortbread history:** Shortbread cookies are ancient and are attributed to Scotland. According to legend, the Scots baked shortbread in the winter months and put cuts into the shortbread rounds to symbolize the sun's rays.

**Makes:** 8 to 12 wedges

# Brown Sugar Shortbread

*These are slice-and-bake shortbreads. Keep a roll of the cookie dough in the refrigerator or freezer for whenever you would like a dozen or so freshly baked cookies. You can keep the dough in the refrigerator up to one week, or in the freezer up to two months, well wrapped. The low baking temperature yields a toasted flavor to these cookies.*

8 ounces (2 sticks) butter
1 cup firmly packed dark brown sugar
1 teaspoon vanilla extract
2½ cups all-purpose flour

In a large bowl, cream the butter and the sugar until well blended. Add the vanilla and flour, beating until smooth. Shape the dough into a 1½-inch-thick roll, wrap in plastic wrap, and refrigerate. If desired, wrap the roll of dough in a top layer of foil and freeze for later use.

**To bake:** Preheat oven to 300°F. Line a baking sheet with parchment paper. Cut the chilled dough into ¼-inch-thick slices and place on the baking sheet about 2 inches apart. (Return remaining dough, wrapped, to the refrigerator.) Bake for 20 minutes until very lightly browned.

To make **Coconut Shortbread Cookies,** replace the brown sugar with ¼ cup white sugar and add 2 cups sweetened flaked coconut to the dough.

**Makes:** 3½ dozen cookies

# Chocolate Chip Platter Cookies

*Chocolate chip cookies are an all-time favorite. One way to speed up the baking process is to bake the dough on a pizza pan and cut it up after baking into either triangles or squares. If you follow the directions for the refrigerator cookie version, you will have cookie dough similar to the kind you can buy. Just cut off as many squares as you would like and bake them. Wrap and refrigerate the remainder of the dough. You can keep the dough in the refrigerator up to one week, or in the freezer up to two months, well wrapped.*

1¼ cups all-purpose flour

½ teaspoon baking soda

¼ teaspoon salt

4 ounces (1 stick) butter, softened

¼ cup granulated sugar

⅓ cup packed brown sugar

1 teaspoon vanilla extract

1 large egg

1 cup (6-ounce package) semisweet chocolate chips

1 cup chopped nuts (optional)

Preheat the oven to 375°F. Coat a 12-inch pizza pan or a 13 x 9-inch rimmed cookie sheet with cooking spray.

In a mixing bowl, mix the flour, baking soda, and salt. Add butter, granulated sugar, and brown sugar to the dry ingredients, and use a hand mixer to mix until blended. Add the vanilla and egg and beat at low speed to make a stiff cookie dough. Mix in the chocolate chips and nuts.

Press out the dough on the prepared pan until evenly thick. Pierce all over with a fork. Bake for 20 to 25 minutes or until golden brown. With a straight-edged knife, cut the warm cookie into triangles or 2-inch squares. Cool in the pan on a wire rack.

**Refrigerator Chocolate Chip Cookies:** Prepare dough and shape into a rectangular cake about 9 x 5 inches and 1 inch thick. Wrap in waxed paper. Refrigerate for 1 hour or until firm. Coat cookie sheet with cooking spray. Preheat oven to 375°F. Cut the rectangle into 1-inch squares and place on cookie sheet about 2 inches apart. Bake for 8 to 10 minutes or until golden brown. Cool for 2 minutes; transfer to wire racks to cool completely. Makes about 45 cookies.

**Makes:** about 4 dozen cookies

# Double Chocolate Chunk Platter Cookies

*Cut these cookies up as you would a pizza, or simply break off pieces. For a birthday party, drizzle cookie with melted chocolate and decorate with candles.*

4 ounces (1 stick) butter, at room temperature

1 (3-ounce) package cream cheese

½ cup packed brown sugar

¼ cup granulated sugar

1 large egg, at room temperature

1 cup all-purpose flour

¼ cup unsweetened cocoa powder

½ teaspoon baking soda

⅛ teaspoon salt

1 (12-ounce) package semisweet chocolate chunks

Preheat the oven to 375°F. Coat a 12-inch pizza pan with cooking spray.

In a large bowl with a hand mixer, cream the butter, cream cheese, brown sugar, and granulated sugar together. Add the egg and beat until fluffy. In another bowl, stir the flour, cocoa, baking soda, and salt together. Add to the creamed mixture, mixing until the dough is stiff. Sir in the chocolate chunks. Press dough evenly onto the prepared pan, pressing the top down with a fork dipped in water. Bake for 20 to 25 minutes or until light brown around the edges and firm in the center. Cool in the pan on a wire rack. Cut into wedges to serve.

**Double Chocolate Chunk Cookies:** Drop rounded spoonfuls of the dough onto a parchment-covered cookie sheet about 2 inches apart. Bake for 8 to 10 minutes until cookies are lightly browned.

**Makes:** 8 cookie wedges

# One-Bowl Cocoa Bars

*These bars are quick and easy and contain common ingredients. If you don't have buttermilk on hand, simply add 2 tablespoons vinegar to ¾ cup regular milk to make sour milk.*

---

4 ounces (1 stick) butter, softened

1 cup sugar

1 large egg

¾ cup buttermilk or sour milk

1 teaspoon vanilla extract

1½ cups all-purpose flour

½ teaspoon baking soda

½ cup unsweetened cocoa powder

Powdered sugar (optional)

---

Preheat the oven to 350°F. Coat a 13x9-inch pan with cooking spray.

Measure all of the ingredients, in the order given, into a large mixing bowl. With a hand mixer, mix until well blended. Pour into the baking pan and smooth the top. Bake for 22 to 25 minutes until a toothpick inserted in the center comes out clean. Cool on a rack and cut into 24 squares. If desired, dust the top of the baked bars with powdered sugar.

---

For a simple **Mocha Cocoa Frosting,** mix 1½ ounces (3 tablespoons) softened butter, 1 cup powdered sugar, 2 tablespoons unsweetened cocoa, 1½ tablespoons cold coffee, and 1 teaspoon vanilla until smooth. Spread over the top of the cooled brownies.

**Makes:** 24 bars

# Saucepan Brownies

*This is a fudgy version of brownies. All the mixing is done in the same saucepan as you melt the butter and chocolate. Very convenient.*

4 ounces (1 stick) butter

4 ounces unsweetened chocolate

1¾ cups sugar

1½ teaspoons vanilla extract

4 large eggs

1 cup all-purpose flour

1 cup coarsely chopped walnuts (optional)

Preheat the oven to 325°F. Coat a 9-inch square baking pan with cooking spray.

In a 2½-quart saucepan, melt the butter and chocolate together over medium-low heat. Remove from the heat and stir in the sugar and vanilla. Add the eggs, one at a time, beating well after each addition with a wooden spoon. Stir in the flour and walnuts. Spread batter evenly in the prepared baking pan. Bake for about 35 minutes or until the brownies feel dry on top. Let cool in the pan on a rack. Cut into squares.

**Makes:** 16 squares

# Walnut Butterscotch Blondies

*These are called blondies, as these chewy brownie-like bars are made without chocolate. Instead, blondies are flavored with butter and brown sugar.*

½ cup (1 stick) butter, softened

1 cup tightly packed light or dark brown sugar

1 large egg, lightly beaten

1 teaspoon vanilla extract

1 cup all-purpose flour

½ teaspoon baking powder

⅛ teaspoon baking soda

Pinch salt

1 cup chopped walnuts or pecans

Preheat the oven to 350°F. Coat a 9-inch square pan with cooking spray.

In a mixing bowl, whisk together the butter and sugar. Add the egg and vanilla. Stir in the flour, baking powder, baking soda, and salt. Mix until well blended. Add the nuts. Turn the mixture into the prepared baking pan and spread out evenly. Bake for 20 to 25 minutes or until a wooden toothpick inserted in the center comes out clean. Cool and cut into squares.

**Makes:** 16 squares

# Applesauce Bars

*This light-textured spice-cake-like bar is flavored with cinnamon and nutmeg and dotted
with raisins and dates. It goes well with an orange-flavored frosting.*

4 ounces (1 stick) butter, melted

1¼ cups firmly packed light or dark brown sugar

½ cup unsweetened applesauce

1 large egg

1 teaspoon vanilla extract

1¼ cups all-purpose flour

1 teaspoon baking powder

¼ teaspoon baking soda

2 teaspoons ground apple pie spice

½ cup raisins

½ cup chopped nuts

½ cup vegetable oil

Preheat the oven to 350°F. Coat a 13x9-inch baking pan with cooking spray.

Measure all of the ingredients, in the order given, into a large bowl. With a hand mixer at low
speed, mix until well blended, scraping the bowl to be sure every ingredient is incorporated.
Spread batter evenly in the prepared pan. Bake for 25 minutes or until a wooden toothpick
inserted in the center comes out clean. Cool. Spread with Orange Frosting (recipe below) if
desired. Cut into 1½ x 3-inch bars.

Apple pie spice can be found in the spice section of the supermarket. Or, you can make
your own by mixing 1 teaspoon ground cinnamon with ¾ teaspoon ground nutmeg and ¼
teaspoon ground cloves.

**Orange Frosting:** In a small bowl, beat together 2 cups powdered sugar, 1½ ounces
(3 tablespoons) softened butter, 2 tablespoons milk, 1 teaspoon vanilla, and ½ teaspoon
grated orange zest, adding more milk if necessary to make a spreadable frosting.

**Makes:** 24 bars

# Flourless Quick Peanut Butter Cookies

*This looks like a strange recipe, but I found it originally in my mother's "Ladies Aid" cookbook. Lately I have come to know many people who have gluten allergies. This is a perfect solution. It is, however, not for those who have a nut allergy! These simple cookies are ready in fewer than 20 minutes. The finished cookies are even better the second day.*

½ cup natural peanut butter, chunky or smooth

½ cup granulated sugar

1 large egg

Preheat the oven to 350°F. Cover a baking sheet with parchment paper.

In a large bowl, stir together the peanut butter, sugar, and egg until well blended. Drop by rounded teaspoonfuls onto the baking sheet. Flatten slightly with a fork dipped in water. Bake for 10 to 12 minutes. Allow to cool on the pan.

When buying peanut butter, read the label. This recipe works the best with peanut butter that is not sweetened. Too much sugar results in cookies that spread out and get very hard when baked.

**Makes:** 15 cookies

# Irish Oatmeal Brownies

*These are called "brownies" in Ireland, but they are not chocolate, rather a toasted oatmeal bar with a hint of cinnamon. You can feel good about serving these healthy bars. Toasted oatmeal takes on a nutty flavor.*

8 ounces (2 sticks) butter, melted

1 cup packed light or dark brown sugar

4 cups quick-cooking rolled oats

½ cup all-purpose flour

2 teaspoons baking soda

2 teaspoons ground cinnamon

Preheat the oven to 350°F. Coat a 13x9-inch baking pan with cooking spray.

In a large bowl, stir together all of the ingredients until well blended. Turn mixture into the baking pan and pat firmly to make the top smooth. Bake for 15 minutes, then reduce the oven temperature to 300°F. and bake 30 minutes longer. Cut into bars while still warm.

**Makes:** 2½ dozen bars

# Raspberry Butter Cookie Strips

*This butter cookie dough is easy to shape by hand into long strips. I like to use raspberry jam, but apricot jam or strawberry or another red jam will be equally delicious.*

4 ounces (1 stick) butter, softened

¼ cup sugar

¼ teaspoon salt

1 large egg yolk

1¼ cups all-purpose flour

⅓ cup raspberry jam, strained

½ cup powdered sugar

1 tablespoon lemon juice

Preheat the oven to 350°F.

In a large bowl, beat butter, sugar, salt, and egg yolk until smooth. Mix in flour. Divide dough into four equal parts. On a floured surface, with your hands, shape each part of dough into strips about 16 inches long. Place the strips about 2 inches apart on a baking sheet. With the edge of a saucer, press a groove along the length of each strip. Bake 10 minutes.

Fill a heavy plastic bag with the strained jam. Clip the corner of the bag and press jam along the groove of each cookie strip. Return to the oven for 5 to 10 minutes longer or until edges are lightly browned.

In a small bowl, mix the powdered sugar, lemon juice, and enough water to make a glaze. Drizzle over the hot cookies alongside the raspberry filling. While still warm, cut into diagonal cookies 2 inches long.

Although these cookies are delicious just-baked, you can make them a week in advance. Keep them in an airtight container in a cool place. The butter flavor intensifies as the cookies age.

**Makes:** about 2 dozen cookies

# Make-Ahead Desserts

Put these into the freezer or fridge a day or a few hours ahead

- Blender Chocolate Pots De Crème
- Chocolate Raspberry Dessert
- Frozen Lemonade Dessert
- Lemon Cheesecake Squares
- Ricotta Ginger Cheesecake
- Fudge-Topped Cheesecake Bars
- Ice Cream Brownie Fudge Torte
- Easy Cranberry Pudding with Quick Brandy Butter Sauce
- Panna Cotta

- Banana Panna Cotta with Kiwi Garnish
- Pumpkin Squares with Gingersnap Crust
- Chilled Apricot Pudding
- Chilled Pear Soup with Port
- Eggnog Angel Cake
- English Trifle
- Maple Pecan Ice Cream Balls
- No-Cook Tiramisù

# Blender Chocolate Pots De Crème

*The blender makes this so simple to put together. The custards need to chill thoroughly before serving.*

1 (6-ounce) package semisweet chocolate chips
1 large egg
2 tablespoons sugar
1 teaspoon vanilla extract
¼ teaspoon salt
1 cup half-and half or whole milk
Whipping cream for serving

Preheat the oven to 325°F. Place 6 custard cups or demitasse cups in a large baking pan.

In a blender, combine the chocolate chips, egg, sugar, vanilla, and salt. Heat cream or milk to the boiling point. Turn blender on and pour the hot cream in through the top opening of the blender cap. Blend at low speed until smooth, about 1 minute. Divide the mixture between the prepared cups. Place the filled cups into a baking pan large enough to accommodate them (a 13x9-inch pan works well). Place baking pan with the filled cups into the preheated oven and carefully pour hot water into the pan halfway up the sides of the cups. Bake until just set, about 25 minutes. Remove from the oven, cool, then refrigerate at least 2 hours or up to 2 days. Serve with whipped cream topping.

To make **White Chocolate Pots De Crème,** substitute 6 ounces white chocolate for the semisweet chocolate chips.

**Serves:** 6

# Chocolate Raspberry Dessert

*Raspberries and chocolate have a special affinity to one another. While this dessert is perfectly delicious without the berries, the combination of the two together raises this dessert up over the top.*

1½ cups fine chocolate cookie crumbs (either chocolate wafers or filled cookies)

**Filling:**

3 tablespoons cornstarch

2 cups milk

2 cups semisweet chocolate chips

1 tablespoon butter

**Topping:**

2 cups fresh raspberries

1 cup chilled heavy whipping cream

2 tablespoons powdered sugar

1 teaspoon vanilla extract

Press the cookie crumbs into the bottom of a lightly buttered 8- or 9-inch square pan. In a small bowl or measuring cup, mix the cornstarch and ¼ cup of the milk; set aside. In a 1-quart saucepan, combine the remaining milk and chocolate chips. Place over medium-high heat and stir until the mixture comes to a boil and the chocolate is melted. Stir the cornstarch mixture into the boiling mixture. Cook about 2 minutes, stirring, until the pudding boils and thickens. Stir in the butter. Spread the pudding over the crumb layer in the pan. Press plastic wrap onto the pudding to cover and chill overnight.

Remove plastic wrap. Top with ¾ of the raspberries, pointed side up, pressing lightly into the pudding. In a medium bowl, beat cream, sugar, and vanilla until stiff. Spread on top of the raspberries. Arrange the remaining berries on top of the cream. Chill up to 2 hours until ready to serve. Cut into squares to serve.

Have the crumb crusts in your freezer all ready to go for a real time-saver.

**Serves:** 9

# Frozen Lemonade Dessert

*Make this dessert in advance and have it ready in the freezer. When you are ready to serve, you'll need to let it stand at room temperature for 10 minutes to make it easier to cut. Return the remaining dessert to the freezer, but be sure to pack it in an airtight container, and serve within two weeks for the best flavor.*

3 cups fine vanilla wafer crumbs
4 ounces (1 stick) butter, melted
1 quart vanilla ice cream, softened
1 (6-ounce) can frozen lemonade concentrate, thawed

Mix the vanilla wafer crumbs with the melted butter. Press half the crumbs into the bottom of an 8- or 9-inch square cake pan. In a medium bowl, mix the ice cream and lemonade concentrate until blended. Spoon into the crust; pack well, smooth the top, and sprinkle with the remaining vanilla wafer crumbs. Cover with plastic wrap and freeze for 4 hours until firm. Wrap well in foil to store. Cut into squares to serve.

 This dessert goes together in minutes. You may use half of a 12-ounce can of frozen, thawed lemonade concentrate – or make 2 desserts.

For a pretty pink pie, use pink lemonade.

**Makes:** 32 to 36 squares

# Lemon Cheesecake Squares

*Who doesn't like cheesecake? The flavor of fresh lemon juice and freshly grated lemon zest pique the flavor of the velvety cream cheese filling. Preparation time here is minimal.*

1½ cups fine graham cracker crumbs

2 ounces (½ stick) butter, softened

1 (8-ounce) package regular cream cheese

2 large eggs

½ cup sugar

1 teaspoon vanilla extract

1 teaspoon freshly grated lemon zest

2 tablespoons freshly squeezed lemon juice

Whipped cream for serving (optional)

Preheat the oven to 350°F. Coat an 8- or 9-inch square pan with cooking spray.

In a medium-sized bowl, mix the graham cracker crumbs and butter. Press in an even layer in the bottom of the pan. In a large mixing bowl, with a hand mixer, beat the cream cheese until smooth and creamy. Beat in the eggs one at a time. Beat in the sugar, vanilla, lemon zest, and lemon juice until the mixture is light. Pour mixture into the crumb-lined pan. Bake for 20 to 25 minutes or until filling is set. Cool. Chill at least 1 hour or overnight. Serve with whipped cream, if desired.

 **Orange Cheesecake Squares:** Flavor the creamy filling with 2 teaspoons grated orange zest in place of the lemon and add 2 tablespoons orange juice concentrate in place of the lemon juice.

To reduce calories and fat, use Neufchâtel or low-fat cream cheese.

To freeze, wrap well in foil, and label and date. Freeze up to 1 month before serving.

**Serves:** 8

# Ricotta Ginger Cheesecake

*Not just low in fat, this delicious cheesecake can be made up to two days ahead and kept chilled.*

⅔ cup fine gingersnap cookie crumbs

1 ounce (2 tablespoons) butter, melted

1 (15-ounce) carton low-fat ricotta cheese

4 large egg whites

Juice and zest of 1 lemon

2 (8-ounce) packages nonfat or low-fat cream cheese

1 cup sugar

½ cup minced crystallized ginger, divided

1 teaspoon vanilla extract

Fruit for garnish: raspberries, strawberries, or sliced kiwi or orange sections

Preheat the oven to 350°F.

In a mixing bowl, combine the crumbs and butter. Pat mixture evenly into the bottom of an 8- or 9-inch springform pan. In a food processor or a large bowl, blend the ricotta cheese, egg whites, lemon juice and zest, cream cheese, sugar, half of the ginger, and vanilla until very smooth. Pour into the crust. Sprinkle remaining ginger over the top. Bake until the center of the cheesecake barely jiggles when gently shaken, 50 to 55 minutes. Cool on a rack for 15 minutes. Run a thin-bladed knife between cheesecake and pan rim but do not remove the rim. Refrigerate, uncovered, until cool, at least 2½ hours. (If making ahead, wrap airtight when cool and chill up to 2 days.)

Before serving, garnish the top of the cheesecake with sliced berries or fruit.

This is a good way to use up any extra egg whites you have on hand. If you wish, you can substitute 2 large eggs for the 4 whites. Crystallized ginger has been cooked in a sugar syrup and coated with sugar. It can be found in the produce section of a well-stocked supermarket.

**Serves:** 12 to 16

# Fudge-Topped Cheesecake Bars

*Think of these bars when you need a big bunch of desserts or are planning to bring dessert to a potluck. They are easy to make and are finished with chocolate fudge ice cream sauce. They take only 15 minutes to prepare, but need 45 minutes to bake and at least 4 to 5 hours to chill.*

1½ cups fine chocolate cookies crumbs (either chocolate wafers or filled cookies)

2 ounces (½ stick) butter, melted

2 pounds (4 8-ounce packages) cream cheese, softened

1 cup sugar

1 cup dairy sour cream

3 tablespoons all-purpose flour

1 tablespoon vanilla extract

4 large eggs

½ cup chocolate fudge ice cream sauce, warmed

Preheat the oven to 325°F. Coat a 13x9-inch baking pan with cooking spray.

Mix the cookie crumbs and melted butter and press evenly into the baking pan. In a large bowl, using a hand mixer, beat the cream cheese and sugar until blended. Add the sour cream, flour, vanilla, and eggs, and beat at low speed until blended. Pour over the crumb crust. Bake for 45 to 55 minutes or until center is just set. Chill for 4 to 5 hours or over-night. Cut into squares and drizzle with the fudge topping before serving.

You can make these delicious squares up to 4 days ahead or freeze them up to 2 weeks ahead. To thaw, remove from the freezer and refrigerate overnight.

**Serves:** 16

# Ice Cream Brownie Fudge Torte

*This family favorite looks fancy but is super simple to put together. It makes two thin layers, which you can bake ahead of time, fill, wrap, and keep it in the freezer until you are ready to serve. This is great for a birthday party!*

4 ounces unsweetened chocolate

8 ounces (2 sticks) butter

4 large eggs

2 cups sugar

2 teaspoons vanilla extract

1 cup all-purpose flour

¼ teaspoon salt

1 cup chopped walnuts (optional)

1 quart vanilla ice cream, softened

Preheat the oven to 325°F. Line 2 (9-inch) round cake pans with parchment paper, and coat lightly with cooking spray.

In a medium saucepan over low heat, melt the chocolate with the butter, stirring constantly. Cool.

With a whisk, beat in the eggs, sugar, and vanilla. Stir in the flour, salt, and walnuts (if using) until well blended. Divide the batter between the two cake pans. Bake for 30 to 35 minutes, until cakes test done when touched in the center. Turn out onto a rack and cool completely.

To finish the torte, place one of the layers on a serving plate and spread with half the softened ice cream. Top with the second layer of cake. Spread remaining ice cream on top. Wrap in foil and keep in freezer until ready to serve. Cut into wedges to serve.

Instead of vanilla ice cream, fill the torte with mint-flavored ice cream and drizzle the torte with chocolate sauce before serving.

**Serves:** 12

# Easy Cranberry Pudding with Quick Brandy Butter Sauce

*Although this pudding does bake for an hour, this delicious dessert is worth it because it is so simple to stir up. You can make the brandy sauce while the pudding bakes.*

**Pudding:**

2 cups fresh cranberries, rinsed and drained

1½ cups all-purpose flour

½ teaspoon salt

½ teaspoon baking soda

⅓ cup boiling water

½ cup light or dark molasses

**Sauce:**

1 cup sugar

4 ounces (1 stick) butter, softened

½ cup heavy whipping cream

2 tablespoons brandy

Preheat the oven to 350°F. Lightly grease a 9x5-inch bread pan.

In a large bowl, stir the cranberries, flour, salt, soda, water, and molasses together until blended. Spoon into the bread pan and cover tightly with a double layer of foil. Place into a larger pan. Set in the oven and carefully pour boiling water to about halfway up the sides of the pudding pan. Bake for 1 hour. Remove from water and allow to cool. When ready to serve, invert onto a serving plate. Cut into 1-inch slices.

**To make the sauce,** mix together the sugar, butter, and cream. Cook over medium heat until thick, about 10 minutes, stirring frequently. Add the brandy and pour sauce over individual slices of the pudding.

This is a perfect dessert to consider when you're pinched for time before an autumn holiday dinner. Just stir up the pudding, bake it, and while it bakes stir the ingredients for the sauce in a saucepan and place over low heat to cook until you are ready to serve the pudding. To make the pudding ahead, bake, cool, remove from the baking pan, and wrap tightly in foil. Refrigerate up to 2 days or freeze up to 2 weeks. If frozen, remove from the freezer 2 hours before serving.

**Serves:** 8 to 10

# Panna Cotta

*Panna cotta is a simple, classic, creamy Italian dessert thickened with gelatin. It can be made up to two days ahead and kept refrigerated. It is delicious served with raspberries or blackberries.*

2 cups (1 pint) half-and-half
1 envelope (¼ ounce) unflavored gelatin
⅓ cup sugar
Pinch salt
1 teaspoon vanilla extract
1 pint fresh raspberries or blackberries (optional)

Pour 1 cup of the half-and-half into a medium saucepan and sprinkle the gelatin on top. Place pan over low heat and stir until the gelatin is dissolved. Let sit for about 5 minutes. Remove from the heat and add the remaining cream, the sugar, and salt and stir until the sugar dissolves. Stir in the vanilla.

Coat 4 (6-ounce) ramekins or custard cups with cooking spray. Strain the mixture into the ramekins. Cover each with plastic wrap and refrigerate for at least 2 hours until firm.

To serve, run a thin knife around the edge of the cups and invert onto dessert dishes. Surround with fresh berries, if desired, and serve.

**Serves:** 4

# Banana Panna Cotta with Kiwi Garnish

*When bananas are flecked with brown, but not yet overripe, they are flavorful and perfect for this easy dessert. This recipe can be made two days ahead and kept refrigerated.*

1 envelope (¼ ounce) unflavored gelatin

¼ cup water

⅓ cup fresh lime juice

1 teaspoon lime zest

¾ cup sugar

1¼ cups half-and-half

1 cup mashed ripe bananas

4 kiwi fruit, peeled and sliced

In a medium-sized metal bowl, combine the gelatin and water. Stir until gelatin is softened. Place bowl over a pot of boiling water and stir until gelatin is dissolved and clear. Slowly add the lime juice, lime zest, and sugar; whisk until well blended. Add the half-and-half and the bananas and mix well.

Coat 6 (4- to 5-ounce) custard cups or ramekins with cooking spray. Divide the banana mixture between the cups. Cover with plastic wrap and chill for 2 hours or until set.

To serve, loosen edges of the panna cotta with a thin knife and turn out onto serving dishes. Top with slices of kiwi fruit and serve.

**Serves:** 6

# Pumpkin Squares with a Gingersnap Crust

*A spicy gingersnap crust and crumb topping gives texture to each bite of this dessert. Consider serving it for a crowd in place of pumpkin pie. You can make this dessert up to four days in advance. Keep it covered in the refrigerator.*

3 cups fine gingersnap cookie crumbs

3 ounces (6 tablespoons) melted butter

½ cup brown sugar

1 (29-ounce) can pumpkin puree

4 large eggs

1½ cups granulated sugar

1 (12-ounce) can evaporated milk

1 tablespoon ground pumpkin pie spice

1 teaspoon vanilla extract

Whipped cream for serving

Preheat oven to 350°F.

In a large bowl, mix the gingersnap crumbs with the melted butter and brown sugar. Press half of the crumb mixture into a 13x9-inch pan. Mix the pumpkin, eggs, sugar, evaporated milk, pumpkin pie spice, and vanilla until well blended. Pour the mixture into the gingersnap crust. Top with remaining gingersnap crumb mixture. Bake for 40 to 45 minutes until set. Remove from the oven and cool on a rack. Refrigerate until cold. Cut into squares and serve with whipped cream.

Pumpkin pie spice is a convenient mixture found in the spice section of supermarkets. To make your own, you can use 1 teaspoon each of cinnamon, nutmeg, and ginger.

**Serves:** 12 to 16

# Chilled Apricot Pudding

*Keep dried apricots on hand for this easy, light, yet richly flavored dessert. For super-quick cooking, use the microwave method. This dessert can be made up to four days in advance.*

1 cup dried apricots

1 cup white wine such as Riesling or white grape juice

1½ cups water

⅓ cup sugar

1 stick cinnamon

Zest from ½ orange (use a potato peeler for large pieces)

Cream or vanilla-flavored nonfat yogurt for serving

In a 2-quart saucepan, combine all of the ingredients except for the cream or yogurt. Bring to a boil over medium-high heat and simmer for 20 to 25 minutes until apricots are puffy. Remove from the heat. Pick out the cinnamon stick and orange zest. Turn remaining mixture, including the juices, into a blender. Process until smooth.

Turn into a serving dish, cover, and refrigerate until ready to serve. Pour cream or spoon vanilla-flavored yogurt over each serving.

 To cook in the microwave, combine the first six ingredients in a large microwave-safe bowl. Microwave on high power for 10 minutes. Proceed as directed.

**Serves:** 4 to 6

# Chilled Pear Soup with Port

*Cooked and pureed, pears make a pretty, pink, silky-smooth, refreshing dessert. It is delicious with a swirl of heavy cream. Perfectly ripe pears should have slight "give" to them when pressed at the core end.*

1 cup port wine

1½ cups water

⅓ cup sugar

Zest from ½ orange

4 black peppercorns

1½ teaspoons star anise seeds

6 medium, firm but ripe Bartlett pears, peeled, halved, cored, and quartered

Heavy cream for serving, if desired

Fresh mint sprigs (for garnish)

In a large 3- or 4-quart saucepan, combine port wine, water, sugar, orange zest, peppercorns, and anise seeds. Bring to a boil, then reduce heat to low and simmer for 5 minutes. Add pear quarters to the hot liquid and gently simmer for 20 to 25 minutes until tender. Remove from heat. Remove the pears from the liquid and place into a blender. Strain the poaching liquid and discard the spices. Put the strained liquid into the blender with the pears and process until pears are pureed and smooth. Chill. When ready to serve, pour the chilled pear soup into six serving dishes. Garnish with mint sprigs.

Star anise seeds are star-shaped, dark brown pods that contain a pea-sized seed in each of its eight segments. Even though star anise is not related to anise, it has a similar licorice flavor and is widely used in Asian cooking. It is one of the ingredients in Chinese five-spice powder. Star anise adds a mild licorice flavor to mulled wine or apple juice. You can find it in Asian markets and some supermarkets

**Serves:** 6

# Eggnog Angel Cake

*This cake can be made ahead and either refrigerated or frozen. If you freeze it, fill the cake before you freeze, but frost with the whipped cream after thawing. Remove the cake from the freezer two hours before serving. The eggnog flavor comes from the rum and nutmeg used in the filling.*

1 (10-inch) angel food cake (baked from a mix or purchased)

**Filling:**

4 ounces (1 stick) butter, softened

2 cups unsifted powdered sugar

1 teaspoon vanilla extract

⅓ cup light rum or ⅓ cup milk and ½ teaspoon rum flavoring

½ teaspoon ground nutmeg

**Frosting:**

2 cups (1 pint) heavy whipping cream

2 tablespoons unsifted powdered sugar

1 teaspoon vanilla extract

Cut the cake into 4 equal layers. For the eggnog-flavored filling, cream the butter with the powdered sugar until light. Add the vanilla, rum, and nutmeg. Beat until fluffy. Spread the filling between the layers of the cake. At this point you can freeze the cake, well wrapped, to serve up to a week later.

A few hours before serving, remove cake from the freezer and unwrap. After the cake has thawed, whip the cream until stiff and fold in the 2 tablespoons powdered sugar and 1 teaspoon vanilla. To frost, spread the sweetened whipped cream over the top and sides of cake.

To make a **Chocolate Cream Angel Cake,** melt 2 squares (2 ounces) unsweetened chocolate with the butter. Cool and add the powdered sugar, vanilla, rum, and nutmeg.

**Serves:** 12

# English Trifle

*A classic dessert in England, trifle consists of a sponge cake, usually doused in sherry, covered with jam and a vanilla-flavored custard, topped with fruit and whipped cream. The trifle may consist of several layers. It's best made ahead and refrigerated. An English cook is so accustomed to making this dessert that she could probably make it in her sleep!*

1 recipe Vanilla Pudding (recipe page 64)

1 (9-inch) sponge cake or frozen pound cake, in ½-inch slices

½ cup sweet sherry

½ cup seedless raspberry jam

3 cups mixed fresh berries (sliced strawberries, raspberries, blackberries)

2 kiwi fruit, peeled and cut into chunks

2 bananas, peeled and cut into chunks

1 cup heavy whipping cream

2 tablespoons powdered sugar

Fresh strawberries for garnish

Prepare the vanilla pudding and set aside to cool. Line the bottom of a glass trifle dish with sponge cake slices. Sprinkle with sherry and spread with the jam. Top with the berries, kiwi, and bananas. Pour the cooled pudding over the fruit and refrigerate, covered, for 4 hours. Before serving, whip the cream to make soft peaks. Beat in the powdered sugar and continue beating until stiff. Spread whipped cream over the top of the trifle and garnish with strawberries.

The classic trifle dish is glass with straight sides so that the layers are visible.

For the fruit or berries, use whatever you have on hand and in season. Peeled, diced stone fruits such as peaches or apricots make delicious substitutes for berries.

**Serves:** 6 to 8

# Maple Pecan Ice Cream Balls

*Make these in advance and keep them in the freezer for a delicious last-minute dessert. Well wrapped, they will keep for about two weeks. Any longer, and the ice cream might develop icy crystals.*

1 pint vanilla ice cream
½ cup finely chopped, toasted pecans
½ cup real maple syrup

Scoop the ice cream into 4 balls, using ½ cup ice cream for each. Roll balls in pecans and serve right away or freeze until ready to serve.

To serve, place ice cream balls into serving dishes and drizzle with 2 tablespoons maple syrup each.

**Honey Sunflower Ice Cream Balls:** Roll vanilla ice cream balls in toasted, salted sunflower nuts and serve with honey.

**Butter Brickle – Chocolate Cookie Crumb Ice Cream Balls:** Roll butter brickle ice cream balls in chocolate cookie crumbs and serve with chocolate sauce.

**Serves:** 4

# No-Cook Tiramisù

*The basic ingredients for authentic tiramisù don't vary much. Mascarpone cheese, eggs, sugar, espresso coffee, ladyfingers, coffee liqueur, and cocoa. Because we cannot use raw eggs these days, this recipe has been altered. This version consists of one delicious layer after another. There is no cooking involved and that will help keep your kitchen cool in the blazing heat of summer. Not only that, but this is great made in advance. I suggest raspberries for the fruit garnish on top, but any other summer berry or sliced soft fruit will be delicious, too. You can freeze the dessert up to two weeks.*

1 cup softened mascarpone cheese or 1 (8-ounce) package cream cheese

1 cup powdered sugar

¼ cup coffee liqueur, rum, or brandy

¼ cup espresso

2 teaspoons vanilla extract

36 ladyfingers or vanilla wafers

1 cup heavy whipping cream

¼ cup grated bittersweet chocolate

2 cups (1 pint) fresh raspberries or diced fresh fruit, divided

In a medium-sized bowl with an electric hand mixer, beat the mascarpone or cream cheese with the powdered sugar until smooth. In a separate small bowl, mix the coffee liqueur, espresso, and vanilla. Dip half the ladyfingers or vanilla wafers in the coffee mixture and place in the bottom of a I-quart glass serving dish. Top with the mascarpone mixture. Dip the remaining ladyfingers or vanilla wafers in the remaining coffee mixture and place on top of the creamed mixture. Whip the cream until stiff and spread over the ladyfinger layer. Sprinkle with the grated chocolate. Chill overnight or for at least 4 hours before serving. Top with the raspberries or other fruit before serving.

Mascarpone is an Italian cream cheese that is buttery-rich and ivory-colored. It is made from cow's milk and ranges in texture from clotted cream to room-temperature butter. It can usually be found in the specialty cheese section of supermarkets.

For a nonalcoholic dessert, use a coffee-flavored syrup instead of the liqueur, usually found in the section of the market where coffee is sold.

**Serves:** 6

# In-a-Pinch Pies & Cakes

Make these desserts with ingredients you have on hand

- Crumb Crust for Pies

- No-Bake Fresh Lime Pie

- Crustless Lemon Coconut Custard Pie

- Peanut Butter Pie in a Chocolate Crust

- Norwegian Apple Pie

- Chocolate Mochaccino Moussecakes

- Ice Cream Strawberry Shortcakes

- Lemon Pudding Cake

- Mix-in-the-Pan Double Chocolate Cake

- Quick German Apple Cake

- Raspberry and Pear Tart

- Simple Fresh Plum Upside-Down Cake

- Strawberries and Lemon Cream in a Phyllo Nest

# Crumb Crust for Pies

*This recipe has less fat and sugar than most. This basic pie shell can be either chilled or baked. The baked pie shell will make serving easier, as a chilled crust may stick to the pan.*

1½ cups fine cookie crumbs (graham crackers, chocolate cookies, vanilla wafers, gingersnap, or zwieback)

1 tablespoon sugar

5 tablespoons butter, melted

Mix the crumbs and sugar together; stir in the melted butter. Line a 9-inch pie pan with the mixture and press firmly into place. Chill for 20 minutes, or bake in a 350°F oven for 10 minutes.

Double or triple the recipe and make extra crusts that you can keep in the freezer until you need them. Slip into large, sealable plastic bags or wrap well in foil. Be sure to label and date each one. Well wrapped, the crusts can be frozen up to 2 months before using.

**Makes:** 1 bottom crust

# No-Bake Fresh Lime Pie

*Keep a few crumb crust pie shells in the freezer for this easy-to-make pie, which will set up in the refrigerator or freezer in just a short time. For Key Lime Pie, use freshly squeezed Key limes, which are in season just a few months and available in specialty markets. Key limes are smaller, roundish, and tend to be more yellow than green.*

1 (9-inch) graham cracker crust, frozen (recipe page 50)
1 (8-ounce) package cream cheese, at room temperature
1 (14-ounce) can sweetened condensed milk
1 teaspoon grated lime zest
½ cup freshly squeezed lime juice
Thin slices of fresh lime for garnish

Remove graham cracker crust from the freezer. In a medium-sized mixing bowl with a hand mixer, beat the cream cheese and sweetened condensed milk until blended. Stir in the lime zest and lime juice until evenly blended. Pour into the graham cracker crust and refrigerate for 4 hours or freeze for 1 hour before serving. Garnish the pie with lime slices before serving.

For a **No-Bake Lemon Pie,** substitute lemon zest for the lime zest and lemon juice for the lime juice. Garnish with a thin slice of fresh lemon.

**Serves:** 8

# Crustless Lemon Coconut Custard Pie

*Just stir the ingredients for this lemony dessert together in one bowl, pour the mixture into a pie pan, and bake. Serve it at room temperature, or chill until the next day.*

4 large eggs

1 cup sugar

2 teaspoons grated lemon zest

⅓ cup freshly squeezed lemon juice

1½ cups sweetened flaked coconut

½ cup all-purpose flour

1½ cups half-and-half or whole milk

1 cup heavy whipping cream, whipped and lightly sweetened, to serve (optional)

Preheat the oven to 350°F. Coat a 9- or 10-inch pie pan with cooking spray.

In a large mixing bowl, whisk together the eggs, sugar, lemon zest, lemon juice, coconut, flour, and half-and-half until evenly blended. Pour into the prepared pan. Bake for 30 to 35 minutes or until set. Cool. Cut into wedges to serve. Top with whipped cream if desired.

To reduce fat and calories, use 1 (12-ounce) can evaporated skim milk in place of the half-and-half or milk.

**Serves:** 8

Hold ID... DEM 4935
Hold Until: 11/25/17

LAW Hold Slip
Weeknight desserts

# Peanut Butter Pie in a Chocolate Crust

*If you love the flavor combination of peanut butter and chocolate, this is your pie.*

1 (9-inch) chocolate crumb crust (recipe page 50)

1 cup heavy whipping cream

1 cup plus 2 tablespoons powdered sugar

1 (8-ounce) package cream cheese, at room temperatures

1 cup smooth or crunchy peanut butter

½ cup semisweet chocolate chips

Remove chocolate crumb crust from the freezer. In a medium bowl, whip the cream with 2 tablespoons powdered sugar; set aside. In another bowl, using a hand mixer, mix the cream cheese, peanut butter, and remaining 1 cup powdered sugar together until well blended. Mix the peanut butter mixture with the whipped cream until well blended. Pour into the crust and refrigerate for 4 hours or freeze for 1 hour before serving.

Before serving, put the chocolate chips into a one-cup measure. Microwave at high speed ½ minute at a time until chips are melted. Drizzle the melted chocolate over the pie and cut into wedges to serve.

To add more crunch to this pie, add up to 1 cup coarsely chopped dry-roasted peanuts along with the peanut butter to the filling

**Serves:** 8

# Norwegian Apple Pie

*So easy, so quick! This is truly a pie in a pinch. You simply stir all of these ingredients together and spread the batter in a pie pan. It is more of an apple cake/pudding than a pie, but it has traditionally been called a "pie" in Norway.*

1 egg
¾ cup sugar
1 teaspoon vanilla extract
1 teaspoon baking powder
¼ teaspoon salt
1 teaspoon ground cinnamon
½ cup all-purpose flour
½ cup chopped pecans or walnuts
2 small, tart apples, diced (about 1 cup)
Whipped cream or cinnamon ice cream for serving

Preheat the oven to 350°F. Generously butter a 9-inch pie pan.

In a large bowl, mix together all of the ingredients except for the whipped cream or ice cream. Stir until dry ingredients are no longer visible. Mixture will be stiff. Spoon into the prepared pie pan. Bake 30 minutes or until browned and slightly puffed. To serve, cut hot pie into wedges; top with dollops of whipped cream or ice cream.

**Serves:** 6 to 8

# Chocolate Mochaccino Moussecakes

*This is truly dessert "in a pinch!" Chocolate-loving guests will never guess how quickly and simply you prepared this dessert with ingredients you can keep on hand. Be ready to serve them within 10 minutes after baking. They might look raw when you take them out of the oven, but don't be tempted to bake them longer, as the center sets into a lovely chocolate mousse.*

2 tablespoons instant coffee granules
2 tablespoons milk
8 ounces bittersweet chocolate
4 large eggs, room temperature
¼ cup all-purpose flour
Whipped cream for serving (optional)

Preheat oven to 325°F. Coat 6 custard cups with cooking spray and place on a baking sheet for easiest handling. In a large metal bowl, set over simmering water, stir the coffee granules and milk together until dissolved. Add the chocolate to the bowl and stir until chocolate is melted. Remove the bowl from the simmering water and whisk in the eggs and flour until ingredients are blended. Divide batter between the custard cups. Bake for 17 minutes. Remove from the oven and let stand for 10 minutes. Run a knife around the edge of each dessert and invert onto a serving dish. Serve with whipped cream if desired.

**Serves:** 6

# Ice Cream Strawberry Shortcakes

*Use up melted ice cream to make these easy shortcakes. They are great filled with fresh berries in season or even sliced peaches or apricots.*

1 cup melted vanilla ice cream
1 cup self-rising flour
6 teaspoons sugar
2 cups (1 pint) fresh strawberries, sliced
3 tablespoons sugar
1 cup heavy whipping cream, whipped

Preheat the oven to 350°F. Cover a baking sheet with parchment paper.

In a medium-sized bowl, stir together the ice cream and flour to make a biscuitlike dough. Scoop dough into 6 equal-sized mounds, place them on the parchment-covered baking sheet, and flatten slightly. Sprinkle each mound with about 1 teaspoon sugar. Bake for 18 to 20 minutes until golden. Remove from the oven and cool.

For shortcakes, split the cakes horizontally and place onto serving dishes. Mix the sliced berries with the 3 tablespoons sugar and spoon onto the bottom of each split cake. Place the top of the shortcake onto the strawberries and top with whipped cream.

If you do not have self-rising flour, use all-purpose flour and add 1 teaspoon baking powder and ¼ teaspoon salt to the recipe.

Substitute your favorite flavor of ice cream — any flavor works well in this recipe.

**Serves:** 6

# Lemon Pudding Cake

*This is a favorite old-fashioned dessert that ends up with a delicate cake on top and a lemon pudding on the bottom.*

1½ cups sugar, divided

½ cup all-purpose flour

¼ teaspoon salt

3 large eggs, separated

1½ cups milk (whole, 2%, or skim)

2 teaspoons grated lemon zest

¼ cup fresh lemon juice

1 ounce (2 tablespoons) butter, melted

Preheat the oven to 350°F. Coat a shallow two-quart casserole or soufflé dish with cooking spray.

In a medium bowl, mix 1 cup of the sugar with the flour and salt. In a separate bowl, stir the egg yolks and milk together, then add to the flour mixture along with the lemon zest and juice.

Whip the egg whites until stiff and add the remaining ½ cup sugar. Fold into the egg yolk mixture. Pour into the casserole dish and set in a larger pan. Drizzle the melted butter over the cake before baking — do not mix it in. Place cake into the oven and pour hot water into the larger pan to about 1 inch depth. Bake for 45 minutes or until the pudding cake is browned on top. To serve, scoop the pudding onto a serving dish and spoon the pudding from the bottom of the dessert over the top. This cake is best served warm.

Although it isn't absolutely necessary, you can "gild the lily" here by topping this dessert with lightly sweetened whipped cream.

**Serves:** 6

# Mix-in-the-Pan Double Chocolate Cake

*This was called "Crazy Cake" in old church ladies' cookbooks because all the ingredients are mixed right in the baking pan.*

3 cups all-purpose flour

2 cups sugar

½ teaspoon salt

2 teaspoons baking soda

½ cup unsweetened cocoa powder

¾ cup vegetable oil

2 tablespoons white or cider vinegar

1 tablespoon vanilla extract

2 cups cold coffee

1 cup semisweet chocolate chips

Preheat the oven to 350°F.

In a 13x9-inch ungreased cake pan, measure the flour, sugar, salt, baking soda, and cocoa. Stir together with a fork. Make three wells in the dry ingredients. Pour the oil into one well, the vinegar into the second, and vanilla into the third. Pour the cold coffee over all and stir with a fork until everything is evenly mixed. Sprinkle chocolate chips evenly over the top. Put the cake into the oven and bake for 30 to 35 minutes or until a wooden toothpick inserted into the center of the cake comes out clean.

You can substitute plain water for the cold coffee, and melted butter for the vegetable oil. If you substitute white chocolate chips for the semisweet chips, the cake ends up with a polka-dot texture.

**Serves:** 12 to 16

# Quick German Apple Cake

*The batter bakes up around the apple slices to make a pretty design. Cinnamon sugar and almonds add flavor and crunch.*

4 ounces (1 stick) butter, at room temperature

¾ cup sugar, divided

3 large eggs

1 teaspoon vanilla extract

1 cup all-purpose flour

1 large apple, peeled, cored, and cut into ¼-inch wedges

1 teaspoon ground cinnamon

¼ cup slivered almonds

Preheat the oven to 375°F. Butter a 9-inch round cake pan.

In a large bowl with a hand mixer, cream the butter and ½ cup of the sugar until light. Beat in the eggs until the mixture is fluffy. Stir in the vanilla and flour, mixing well. Spread batter evenly into the buttered pan. Push apple wedges into the batter to form a circular pattern. Mix the remaining ¼ cup sugar with the cinnamon and sprinkle over the cake. Sprinkle the top with the almonds. Bake for 40 minutes or until a wooden toothpick inserted in the center comes out clean. Cut into wedges and serve at room temperature.

This dessert is similar to a German and Austrian favorite, often called "kuchen," which when translated simply means "cake."

**Serves:** 8

# Raspberry and Pear Tart

*Keep a package of frozen puff pastry in the freezer when you suspect you might need a quick, last minute dessert. The pastry will keep, thawed, in the refrigerator up to two days. With four simple ingredients you can put these elegant-looking rustic tarts together and bake them for a quick dessert. Top tarts off with a small scoop of ice cream if you wish.*

1 sheet frozen puff pastry
4 tablespoons raspberry jam
2 large ripe pears, peeled, cored, and thinly sliced
Cinnamon sugar

Preheat the oven to 400°F. Cover a baking sheet with parchment paper.

Thaw the pastry dough and cut into 4 equal rectangles. Place the squares on the parchment covered baking sheet. Spoon 1 tablespoon raspberry jam onto the center of each of the rectangles. Place the pear slices in a tight, overlapping fashion on top of the raspberry jam. Sprinkle lightly with cinnamon sugar. Turn the edges of the pastry upward and pinch the corners. Bake for 20 minutes until pastry is golden. Let cool on the baking sheet. Serve slightly warm or at room temperature.

How to handle frozen puff pastry: Remove as many pastry sheets as needed from the package. Wrap unused pastry in plastic wrap or foil and return to freezer. For quick thawing, cover the pastry with a piece of plastic wrap and let thaw at room temperature for about 30 minutes. Or, place in the refrigerator and use in about 4 hours.

**Serves:** 4

# Simple Fresh Plum Upside-Down Cake

*Use any variety of fresh plums when they come into season at the end of the summer and early fall.*

4 firm, ripe plums, pitted and quartered (if plums are large, cut into eighths)

¼ cup plus ⅔ cup sugar

1 cup all-purpose flour

1 teaspoon baking powder

¼ teaspoon salt

4 ounces (1 stick) butter, softened

1 large egg

⅔ cup milk (whole, 2%, or skim)

1 teaspoon vanilla extract

Whipped cream for serving

Preheat the oven to 350°F. Line a 9-inch round cake pan with parchment paper.

Arrange plums in the bottom of the pan, cut-side up. Sprinkle with ¼ cup of the sugar.

Combine the remaining ingredients, except for the whipped cream, in a large mixing bowl. With a hand mixer at low speed, mix, scraping the sides of the bowl often, until the batter is smooth. Pour the batter over the plums and bake for 45 to 50 minutes or until the cake feels firm when touched in the center. Run a butter knife around the edge of the cake to loosen. Place a rimmed serving plate over the top and invert the cake onto the plate. (The rim will catch the juices.) Pull away the parchment paper. Cut into wedges to serve warm, topped with whipped cream.

For different fruit flavors, replace plums with halved and pitted fresh peaches, or fresh or canned pineapple slices, or fresh or canned pitted cherries.

**Serves:** 6 to 8

# Strawberries and Lemon Cream in a Phyllo Nest

*You can impress your guests with this elaborate-looking, but simple-to-make pie.*

20 sheets (8 ounces) phyllo dough, thawed

2 ounces (½ stick) butter, melted

2 tablespoons sugar

**Filling:**

1 (8-ounce) tub mascarpone

⅓ cup powdered sugar

1 tablespoon grated lemon zest

2 pints fresh strawberries, cleaned, stemmed, and halved

¼ cup strawberry jelly, melted

Preheat the oven to 375°F. Coat a 9-inch pie pan with cooking spray.

Place the phyllo sheets one on top of the other, then roll up jelly-roll style. Cut into ½-inch strips. Place into a bowl and sprinkle with the butter and sugar. Toss until phyllo ribbons are coated. Turn into the pie pan and arrange the strips so that they coat the bottom and sides of the pan. Bake for 12 to 15 minutes, until golden and crisp. Remove from oven and cool on a rack. This can be done several hours ahead.

In a small bowl, mix the mascarpone, powdered sugar, and lemon zest until well blended. Before serving, spoon the mascarpone mixture evenly over the bottom of the baked crust. Combine the strawberries and melted jelly, then arrange strawberries over the lemon cream. Chill until ready to serve or serve right away.

You can fill the nest with any other fresh fruit such as raspberries or sliced and pitted fresh peaches or apricots, glazed with the jelly.

Phyllo (also called filo or fillo) is a translation of the Greek word that means "leaf." We know it as a very thin dough that is similar to a strudel dough. It is available frozen. Unopened, it can be stored for up to a month in the refrigerator, but once opened use it within 2 to 3 days.

**Serves:** 6

# Just Whipped Up Soufflés, Custards & Puddings

Old and new classics come together quickly and deliciously

- Stirred Vanilla Pudding
- Chocolate Rum Pudding Pots
- Peach Custard Desserts
- Baked Chocolate Custard
- Chocolate Soufflé
- Sugared Orange Soufflé

- Salzburger Nockerln
- Mango and Lime Fool
- Blueberry Kissel
- Danish Red Berry Pudding
- Veiled Country Lass

# Stirred Vanilla Pudding

*It is so easy to forget the simplest of puddings, one that hearkens back to childhood comfort food. This pudding takes less than 10 minutes to prepare.*

½ cup sugar

3 tablespoons cornstarch

⅛ teaspoon salt

1 whole large egg or 2 egg yolks

2 cups milk (whole, 2%, or skim)

1 ounce (¼ stick) butter

2 teaspoons vanilla extract

In a saucepan, stir together sugar, cornstarch, salt, and egg. Place over medium heat, and whisk in the milk. Place over low heat, stirring, until mixture boils. Boil 1 minute and blend in the butter and vanilla. Let cool briefly, and serve warm, or chill until ready to serve.

Vanilla pudding is a key ingredient in an English Trifle, and this basic made-from-scratch pudding tastes so much better than instant pudding mixes.

For **Chocolate Pudding,** add ¼ cup more sugar to the pudding and add 2 squares unsweetened chocolate to the hot pudding. Stir until chocolate is melted.

For **Butterscotch Pudding,** replace the white sugar with dark brown sugar.

For **Banana Cream Pudding,** fold 2 sliced bananas into a Butterscotch or Chocolate Pudding along with the vanilla.

For **Coconut Cream Pudding,** stir ½ cup sweetened flaked coconut into the pudding along with the milk. Add ¼ teaspoon almond extract with the vanilla.

For a **Reduced Calorie Pudding,** decrease the sugar to ⅓ cup and use skim milk. Omit the butter.

**Serves:** 4

# Chocolate Rum Pudding Pots

*Rich and chocolaty! You don't need a lot of ingredients or time to produce this delicious pudding from scratch.*

2 cups milk (whole, 2%, or skim)
1 cup semisweet chocolate chips
3 tablespoons cornstarch
4 tablespoons dark rum

In a 1-quart saucepan, heat the milk and chocolate chips together, stirring until the chocolate melts. Mix the cornstarch with the rum and slowly stir into the chocolate mixture. Cook over medium-high heat for 2 to 3 minutes until the mixture thickens. Remove from the heat and pour into four dessert dishes. Serve warm, at room temperature, or chilled.

Layer the finished pudding in parfait glasses with whipped cream to make a fancier dessert and to stretch the yield to 6 or 8 servings.

**Serves:** 4

# Peach Custard Desserts

*This simple but wholesome dessert is perfect for a homey weekday meal. When peaches are in season, use fresh, peeled, pitted, and halved peaches in place of the canned.*

6 canned peach halves, drained

1½ cups milk (whole, 2%, or skim), scalded

2 large eggs, beaten

3 tablespoons sugar

½ teaspoon almond extract

Preheat the oven to 350°F. Have six (6-ounce) custard cups ready and a rimmed baking dish large enough to hold them all, along with about 1 quart of boiling water.

Place a peach half into each of the custard cups. In a deep, 1-quart bowl, whisk together the milk, eggs, sugar, and almond extract. Pour the egg-milk mixture over the peach halves, dividing mixture evenly between the custard cups. Place into the baking dish and set dish into the oven. Carefully pour boiling water into the dish (but not into the custard cups!) to depth of 1 inch. Bake for 25 minutes or until custards are set; shake gently to test. Remove dish from the oven and the custard cups from the dish. Chill if desired, or serve at room temperature.

Even though you can make this dessert 2 or 3 days in advance and serve it chilled, it is good hot out of the oven. The almond extract enhances the flavor of the peaches.

**Serves:** 6

# Baked Chocolate Custard

*This simple chocolate dessert is easy to whip up using ingredients most everyone has on hand. And in my experience, this is always a favorite with children.*

2 cups milk (whole, 2%, or skim)
¾ cup chocolate ice cream syrup
3 large eggs, lightly beaten
¼ cup sugar
1 teaspoon vanilla extract
⅛ teaspoon salt
Heavy whipping cream (optional)

Preheat the oven to 325°F. Have six (5- to 6-ounce) custard cups ready and a rimmed baking dish large enough to hold them all, along with about 1 quart of boiling water for the dish.

Heat the milk in the microwave oven to boiling. In mixing bowl whisk together the chocolate syrup, eggs, sugar, vanilla, and salt; gradually stir in the boiling milk until blended. Strain through a sieve and divide between the custard cups. Set cups in the baking dish. Place into the oven and carefully pour boiling water into the dish around the cups, to depth of 1 inch. Bake at 325°F until a knife inserted just off-center comes out clean, 35 to 45 minutes. Remove cake from the oven and serve warm or cooled with cream to pour over (if using).

If you make these custards ahead, cover and chill them. Otherwise, they are delicious served warm with a light pouring of cream or half-and-half. For the best texture, be careful not to overcook any custard. Overcooked, custards may become watery.

**Serves:** 6

# Chocolate Soufflé

*Eliminating the butter in the basic sauce for this soufflé lowers the calorie count and lets it rise higher and stay up a bit longer than any traditional method. The old adage is still true, "The guests must wait for the soufflé, not the soufflé for the guest."*

Granulated sugar (for coating soufflé dish)

4 ounces sweet or semisweet cooking chocolate, broken

1 tablespoon instant coffee

1⅓ cups milk (whole, 2%, or skim), divided

⅓ cup all-purpose flour

½ teaspoon vanilla extract

6 large eggs, separated

½ cup granulated sugar

Powdered sugar for serving

Preheat the oven to 375°F. Wrap a foil collar around a 1½-quart soufflé dish to extend the sides about 3 inches. Coat the soufflé dish with cooking spray and sprinkle with granulated sugar.

In a small saucepan over low heat, melt the chocolate with the coffee in ⅛ cup milk; set aside. In a medium saucepan, stir the flour with the remaining 1 cup milk until blended. Stir constantly over medium-high heat until thickened and smooth; cook for 1 minute. Remove from heat and stir in the vanilla and chocolate mixture. Beat in the yolks one at a time, beating well after each; set aside. In a large bowl, beat the egg whites until foamy. Gradually beat in the sugar until the mixture forms glossy peaks. Gently fold the whites into the sauce until almost completely blended. Bake for 25 minutes for a saucy center, 35 minutes for a firm center. Remove the collar, sprinkle the soufflé with powdered sugar, and serve right away.

When separating eggs, make sure the whites go into a perfectly clean, dry bowl. The tiniest bit of yolk or grease will keep the whites from beating perfectly.

**Serves:** 6

# Sugared Orange Soufflé

*This is a great dessert to make in the winter and spring when the citrus is in season and plentiful. You can put this soufflé together up to two hours before baking it and just pop it into the oven about a half hour before you're ready to serve dessert.*

Granulated sugar (for coating soufflé dish)

⅓ cup all-purpose flour

1 cup half-and-half or milk

2 teaspoons each grated orange and lemon zest

⅓ cup orange-flavored liqueur or thawed orange juice concentrate

6 large eggs, separated

½ cup granulated sugar

Powdered sugar for serving

Preheat the oven to 375°F. Wrap a foil collar around a 1½-quart soufflé dish to extend the sides about 3 inches. Coat the soufflé dish with cooking spray and sprinkle with granulated sugar.

In a medium saucepan, stir flour with the half-and-half until blended. Over medium-high heat, stir until thickened and smooth; cook for 1 minute. Remove from heat and stir in the zest and liqueur. Beat in egg yolks one at a time, beating well after each addition; set aside. In a large bowl, beat the whites until foamy. Continue beating, adding the sugar gradually until the mixture forms glossy peaks. Gently fold the whites into the sauce until almost completely mixed in. Pour into the prepared soufflé dish. Bake for 25 minutes for a saucy center, 35 minutes for a firm center. Remove collar and sprinkle the soufflé with powdered sugar. Serve right away.

**Serves:** 6

# Salzburger Nockerln

*Subtly sweet, this classic Austrian soufflé-like dessert is not difficult to make, though it can look imposing. You do need to have guests seated at the table when you present the dessert hot from the oven.*

1 tablespoon plus 1 teaspoon unsalted butter

¾ cup granulated sugar, divided

9 large egg whites, at room temperature

4 egg yolks

¼ cup all-purpose flour

Powdered sugar for serving

Lightly whipped cream for serving

Preheat the oven to 450°F. Coat a large shallow platter or baking pan (preferably metal) with the butter, and sprinkle the bottom with 2 tablespoons of the sugar.

In a large mixing bowl, beat the egg whites with an electric mixer until frothy. Slowly add ¼ cup of the remaining sugar and beat until very stiff and glossy.

In another bowl, beat the egg yolks with the remaining sugar until fluffy. Gently fold the beaten yolks and flour into the beaten egg whites.

Using a rubber spatula, place six even mounds of the mixture into the prepared pan. Bake for 8 minutes until the mounds are puffed and golden. Dust with powdered sugar and, using a spatula, transfer the mounds onto six serving dishes. Serve right away with lightly whipped cream.

🔆 A metal baking pan is the best for this dessert because it conducts the heat more quickly in the oven. You can use an ovenproof metal serving platter to bake the dessert if you wish.

**Serves:** 6

# Mango and Lime Fool

*England is the home of the original "fool" — a pureed fruit that is folded into whipped cream. Gooseberries are the classic dessert, but this combination of mango, lime, and cream is superb.*

1 ripe mango
Zest and juice of 1 lime
3 tablespoons plain yogurt
3 tablespoons heavy whipping cream
¼ cup powdered sugar

Peel the mango, and remove the flesh from the seed. Add to a food processor with the lime zest and juice. Process until pureed. Add the yogurt, cream, and powdered sugar to the processor and process until well blended. Spoon into two dessert dishes and chill until ready to serve.

**Serves:** 2

# Blueberry Kissel

*This is probably the favorite dessert in Northern Europe, especially in Finland and Russia. It is a thickened fruit soup, usually made with fresh berries that are in season.*

1½ pounds fresh or frozen blueberries
½ cup, plus 2 tablespoons, sugar
1 cup orange juice
2 teaspoons grated orange zest
2 tablespoons minute tapioca
¼ cup toasted sliced almonds
Whipped cream for serving

In a medium saucepan, combine the blueberries, ½ cup sugar, orange juice, orange zest, and tapioca. Stir well and let stand for 5 minutes. Place over medium-low heat and simmer, stirring occasionally, until the mixture thickens. Pour mixture into a heatproof serving dish. Sprinkle with remaining 2 tablespoons sugar (this prevents a skin from forming on top). Arrange toasted almonds on top. Serve warm or cold with whipped cream. You can make this dessert up to 4 hours before serving; keep it refrigerated.

For **Rhubarb Strawberry Kissel,** substitute chopped fresh rhubarb and strawberries for the blueberries and increase the sugar to 1 cup.

**Serves:** 4 to 6

# Danish Red Berry Pudding

*Whether this is made ahead or at the last minute, the Danes love this dessert. It is generally served chilled with either whipped cream or pouring cream. Butter cookies on the side are a common addition.*

1 pound fresh or frozen unsweetened raspberries, strawberries, blackberries, or boysenberries

About 4 cups water

⅓ cup cornstarch

1 cup sugar

¼ cup toasted sliced almonds

1 cup heavy cream for serving

In a medium saucepan, combine the berries and 4 cups water, or enough to cover the berries. Bring to a boil. Simmer over low heat for 5 minutes. Pour berry mixture into a sieve; press with the back of a spoon to remove as much pulp as possible. Discard seeds. Measure juice and pulp and add water to equal 5 cups.

In a small bowl, combine the cornstarch with ⅔ cup of the juice to make a thin paste. Pour the remaining juice into saucepan. Bring to a boil over medium heat, stirring occasionally. Stir in the sugar and cornstarch paste. Stirring vigorously with a wooden spoon to keep the mixture smooth, cook until thickened. Cover pan and set in a cool place for 20 to 30 minutes.

Pour cooled pudding into a serving bowl. Sprinkle with sliced almonds. Serve immediately or cover bowl with plastic wrap and refrigerate until served. Pour whipping cream into a small pitcher to serve with the pudding.

**Serves:** 8

# Veiled Country Lass

*There are many versions of this classic Norwegian dessert, which is basically applesauce layered with toasted bread crumbs. Cinnamon and ground hazelnuts add wonderful flavor and texture. Although you can serve this dessert in one large glass bowl, it is very nice to prepare it in individual portions.*

2 cups fine, dry bread crumbs, preferably from homemade bread, preferably rye

4 tablespoons superfine sugar

1 tablespoon ground cinnamon

2 ounces (½ stick) butter, melted

2 cups chilled applesauce, preferably homemade

2 cups heavy whipping cream, whipped

½ cup chopped toasted hazelnuts (or filberts)

In a heavy, nonstick skillet, combine the bread crumbs, sugar, cinnamon, and butter. Stir over medium heat until the crumbs are uniformly golden. Remove from heat and cool.

Layer the applesauce, bread crumbs, and cream in a serving bowl or bowls. There should be at least two layers of each. The top layer should always be whipped cream, "veiling" the dish. Sprinkle with the chopped nuts and serve.

**Serves:** 6

# Fresh Fruit Finishes

You can't miss when fresh fruits are in season

- Almond Peach Crisp

- Any Fruit Cobbler

- Baked Jelly Apples

- Banana Push-ups

- Bananas Foster

- Brown Sugar – Broiled Peaches

- Cherries Jubilee

- Cranberries Jubilee

- Cinnamon Oranges with Vanilla Yogurt

- Easy Berry Ice Cream

- Fresh Cranberry Pudding with Rum Butter Sauce

- Frozen Cranberries with Hot Caramel Sauce

- Grilled Fresh Pineapple Slices

- Havana Bananas

- Honey Ambrosia

- Mango Raisin Flambé

- Strawberry and Rhubarb Tart

- Sugar-Baked Pears with Minted Cream

- Tropical Fruits with Sour Cream Ginger Sauce

# Almond Peach Crisp

*Peaches have a natural affinity for the flavor of almonds. The spiced topping is a cross between a crisp and a cobbler.*

4 large, ripe peaches, peeled and sliced
½ cup tightly packed light or dark brown sugar
½ cup all-purpose flour
½ teaspoon ground cinnamon
¼ teaspoon ground nutmeg
2½ ounces (5 tablespoons) firm butter
½ cup slivered or sliced almonds
Heavy cream for serving (optional)

Preheat the oven to 375°F. Butter a 9-inch square pan or a 10-inch shallow round baking pan. Arrange peach slices in the pan. Combine the brown sugar, flour, cinnamon, and nutmeg. Cut in the butter until mixture is crumbly. Sprinkle the mixture over the peaches in the pan and top with the almonds.

Bake for 30 minutes until topping is browned. Let cool briefly and serve warm, or chill until ready to serve. Serve with cream to pour over, if desired.

The difference between a crisp and a cobbler is that the cobbler's top layer is more biscuitlike. Other similar desserts in New England might be called a "grunt" or a "slump," and sometimes the difference may be whether the dish is cooked on the stovetop or in the oven.

**Serves:** 4 to 6

# Any Fruit Cobbler

*While apple is probably the most common fruit used in a cobbler, you can make this favorite dessert using almost any fruit or berry. This cobbler is essentially a sweetened fruit mixture with a rich shortcake topping.*

2 cups fresh, peeled, cored, and chopped apples, peaches, pears, or berries

½ cup sugar, divided

1 tablespoon quick-cooking or minute tapioca

6 ounces (1½ sticks) butter, divided

2 cups all-purpose flour

4 teaspoons baking powder

½ teaspoon salt

1 large egg, slightly beaten

⅓ cup milk

Whipped cream for serving

Preheat the oven to 425°F. Butter a shallow 1½-quart baking dish and spread the fruit in the dish in an even layer. Sprinkle with 1/4 cup of the sugar and the tapioca. Dot with 1 ounce (2 tablespoons) butter.

In a large bowl, combine the flour, baking powder, salt, and ¼ cup sugar. Cut in the remaining butter until the butter is in pea-sized pieces. In a separate bowl, combine the egg and milk, then stir into the flour mixture. Mix together until it forms a dough. Pat dough out to ¾-inch thickness and cut into rounds with a cookie cutter. Place the rounds on top of the fruit mixture in the pan, overlapping if necessary. Bake for 30 minutes or until cobbler is bubbly around the edges. Serve hot, warm, or cooled with whipped cream.

**Serves:** 6

# Baked Jelly Apples

*Golden Delicious apples are the French favorite for baking because they hold their shape. Baked with a glaze of apple jelly, they are perfect served hot with ice cream or simply with heavy cream poured over.*

4 large Golden Delicious apples
4 pitted dates
3 tablespoons sugar
2 teaspoons ground cinnamon
½ cup apple jelly
1 cup apple cider
Heavy cream or ice cream for serving

Preheat the oven to 375°F.

Core the apples and remove a strip of the peel from around the middle of each apple. Push a whole date into each apple. Stand the apples up in a shallow baking dish (cut a thin slice from the bottom of each to help stand them up). Mix the sugar and cinnamon and sprinkle over the apples. In a small saucepan over medium-low heat, heat the jelly and cider to boiling, stirring until the jelly is melted. Drizzle over the apples and bake for 30 minutes or until tender. Spoon pan juices over the apples to serve. Serve hot with cream or ice cream.

**Serves:** 4

# Banana Push-ups

*This is a healthy dessert for kids. Freeze this mixture in little bathroom-size paper cups. Take out as many mini-pops as you need and press from the bottom to push the ice-cream-like treats up.*

2 large, ripe bananas
½ cup dry milk powder
1 cup plain yogurt
1 cup frozen concentrated orange juice, melted
1 cup water

Place 10 (4-ounce) paper cups into a 9x13-inch baking pan.

Peel the bananas, cut them up, and combine in a blender with the milk powder, yogurt, orange juice concentrate, and water. Process until blended and pour into the paper cups. Cover with plastic wrap and place into the freezer. Freeze for at least 4 hours before serving.

**Serves:** 10

# Bananas Foster

*This dessert was created in New Orleans in the 1950s and named after Richard Foster, a regular customer at Brennan's. To get a good flame, use the simple trick of warming the rum before you try to ignite it, and pour the ignited liquor over the bananas in the pan.*

4 bananas

1½ ounces (3 tablespoons) butter

¼ cup brown sugar

½ cup golden or dark rum

Ice cream for serving

Peel the bananas and cut them in halves lengthwise and then again horizontally.

Melt the butter in a medium skillet over medium heat. Stir in the brown sugar until it is dissolved, then add the bananas. Warm the rum slightly in a small pan, then ignite. Pour over the bananas and shake the pan until the flames die down. Transfer banana pieces to individual plates and serve with a scoop of ice cream.

 Select bananas that are ripe but still firm, not mushy, for the best flavor and texture.

**Serves:** 4

# Brown Sugar – Broiled Peaches

*So simple yet delicious — especially when stone fruits (peaches, nectarines, and apricots) are in season and abundant. Plan on a half piece of fruit per serving and serve with cream or ice cream.*

2 medium-sized fresh peaches or nectarines

1 tablespoon brown sugar

Fresh lemon juice, if desired

Whipped cream or vanilla ice cream (optional), for serving

Preheat the broiler. Line a small, shallow baking dish with foil and coat with cooking spray. Wash, dry, and cut the fruit in half; remove the pit or pits. Place peach halves with the cut-side down on a baking pan and broil about 6 inches from the heat for 3 to 4 minutes. Turn the fruit over and sprinkle with the brown sugar. Broil until sugar is melted, another 2 to 3 minutes. Serve a hot peach half per person with whipped cream or ice cream, if desired.

 Tofu ice cream is great for those who are intolerant of lactose.

**Serves:** 4

# Cherries Jubilee

*This is an old-fashioned dessert that is just as appealing today as it ever was. Keep a can of pitted Bing cherries on hand and vanilla ice cream in the freezer, and brandy, cognac, or kirsch on the cupboard shelf. This has hardly any preparation involved!*

2 (15-ounce) cans Bing cherries, or 1 (1-pound) bag frozen pitted Bing cherries, thawed
1 tablespoon sugar
1 tablespoon cornstarch
¼ cup brandy, cognac, or kirsch
1 quart vanilla ice cream for serving

In a skillet or shallow pan, combine the cherries, sugar, and cornstarch. Place over medium heat and stir until the juices come to a boil and thicken.

Pour the brandy in a metal ladle or long-handled cup and place over low heat until brandy is slightly warmed. Ignite the brandy and pour over the cherries in the pan. Shake pan until flames are extinguished. Spoon hot cherries over servings of ice cream.

**Serves:** 8

# Cranberries Jubilee

*Cranberries are a major crop not only in American states, but in Canadian provinces as well as in northern European countries. On the American and Canadian table, cranberries are important on the Thanksgiving menu. In European countries they are part of Winter Festival menus.*

2 cups fresh cranberries, washed
1 cup water
½ cup sugar
2 tablespoons brandy or rum
Ice cream for serving

Combine cranberries, water, and sugar in a 2-quart saucepan. Bring to a boil over high heat and simmer for 8 to 10 minutes until thickened. Remove from the heat. Warm the brandy or rum in a small metal pan. Touch with a lighted match to ignite and pour over the cranberries. Shake pan until flames are extinguished. Spoon hot cranberries over scoops of ice cream.

For a spectacular presentation, put the hot cranberry sauce into a shallow pan and flame it at the table. Offer scoops of ice cream in a bowl. Vanilla is the favorite, but chocolate ice cream works well, too.

**Serves:** 6

# Cinnamon Oranges with Vanilla Yogurt

*This is an "almost instant" dessert that is popular in South America. Sliced navel oranges are sprinkled with cinnamon-sugar to make a refreshing wintertime dessert. Serve the vanilla yogurt like a sauce on the side.*

6 navel oranges, peeled and sliced ¼ inch thick

2 tablespoons powdered sugar

½ teaspoon ground cinnamon

2 teaspoons orange-flower water or orange-flavored liqueur such as Triple Sec

6 pitted dates, thinly sliced

1½ cups vanilla-flavored low-fat yogurt for serving

Arrange the orange slices overlapping on a platter. Mix the powdered sugar and cinnamon and sprinkle evenly over the oranges. Drizzle with the orange-flower water or liqueur. Sprinkle with the dates. Offer the flavored yogurt in a bowl to spoon over the individual servings of the oranges.

Orange-flower water is a natural extract made from the distillation of orange blossoms. It is commonly used in Middle Eastern cooking.

**Serves:** 6

# Easy Berry Ice Cream

*With a blender or a food processor, it's easy to whip up a delicious, creamy, ice cream, and you can keep the calories and fat low, too!*

1 (16-ounce) package frozen raspberries or strawberries
½ cup heavy whipping cream
½ cup vanilla-flavored nonfat yogurt
Sugar, if desired

Combine the frozen berries, cream, and yogurt in a blender or food processor. Process or blend until smooth. Add sugar to taste. Serve immediately or turn into a bowl, cover with foil, and keep in the freezer (up to 24 hours) until ready to serve.

This ice cream can be made with other soft fruits such as pureed peaches, apricots, and mangoes.

**Serves:** 6

# Fresh Cranberry Pudding with Rum Butter Sauce

*Served with the Rum Butter Sauce (recipe page 87), this cranberry pudding is a lovely holiday dessert. The sauce provides a sweet contrast to the tartness of the cranberries. If your cranberries are frozen, allow about 10 minutes more baking time.*

4 ounces (1 stick) butter, softened

1½ cups fresh cranberries

¼ cup coarsely chopped walnuts

¾ cup sugar, divided

1 large egg

½ cup all-purpose flour

Rum Butter Sauce

Preheat the oven to 325°F. Spread 1 ounce (2 tablespoons) of the butter over the bottom and sides of an 8- or 9-inch pie pan. Wash the cranberries and pat dry. Spread them in an even layer in the bottom of the buttered pie pan. Top with the walnuts and half the sugar. In a mixing bowl, beat the egg with the remaining sugar until the mixture is thick and creamy. Add the flour. Melt the remaining butter and add to the batter. Pour batter over the cranberries and nuts. Bake for 45 minutes or until the top is golden and a cake tester comes out clean. Cool to room temperature. Cut into wedges and lift with a pie server onto serving plates, inverting each piece so the cranberries are on top. Serve with the Rum Butter Sauce.

**Serves:** 6

# Rum Butter Sauce

*This is best served hot. If you make it ahead, cover and refrigerate until a few minutes before serving. Return to high heat and stir until sauce comes to a boil.*

1 cup sugar
½ cup heavy whipping cream
4 ounces (1 stick) butter
2 tablespoons rum
2 teaspoons vanilla extract

Combine the sugar, cream, and butter in a 1-quart saucepan. Place over high heat, stirring constantly, and bring mixture to a boil. Boil for 3 minutes, stirring. Remove from heat and add the rum and vanilla.

**Makes:** about 1 cup sauce

# Frozen Cranberries with Hot Caramel Sauce

*Buy extra cranberries when they are in season and freeze them. When you need a spectacular last-minute dessert, make the caramel sauce and serve the boiling hot caramel sauce over the frozen chopped cranberries. Be sure that your serving dishes can handle the extreme temperatures.*

1 cup sugar

1 cup heavy whipping cream

2 teaspoons dark corn syrup

1 tablespoon butter

2 teaspoons vanilla extract

2 cups rinsed, frozen cranberries, coarsely chopped

Immediately before serving, combine the sugar and cream in a heavy saucepan. Place over medium-high heat and bring to a boil, stirring. Boil for 5 minutes or until the sauce is slightly thickened and light tan in color. Add the corn syrup, butter, and vanilla and stir to combine.

Scoop the chopped frozen cranberries into a dessert dish, preferably pottery, and pour the boiling hot syrup over. Serve immediately.

Freeze the cranberries up to several months before you plan to serve them. For easiest handling, freeze them spread in a single layer on a cookie sheet. After the cranberries are frozen solid, you can turn them into a covered container.

**Serves:** 6

# Grilled Fresh Pineapple Slices

*This is a perfectly simple dessert to go with any grilled food such as teriyaki grilled chicken breasts or grilled boneless pork chops. As an alternative, you can broil the pineapple slices, or grill them in a heated cast-iron grill pan on the stovetop.*

1 medium-sized fresh pineapple

About 1 tablespoon flour for dusting pineapple slices

½ cup sugar

1 tablespoon ground cinnamon

¼ cup unsweetened coconut milk

Whipped cream or ice cream for serving

Preheat the grill, broiler, or stovetop grill pan. Coat pan with nonstick spray.

Cut the rind off the pineapple and remove the "eyes" from the outside. Cut into 1-inch thick slices. Dust the slices lightly with flour. Mix the sugar and cinnamon and put into a plate. Pour the coconut milk into another plate. Dip the flour-dusted slices first into the coconut milk, then into the cinnamon sugar, coating both sides of each slice.

Grill or broil for about 6 minutes on each side. Serve immediately on dessert plates topped with a whipped cream or ice cream, if desired.

**Serves:** 6 to 8

# Havana Bananas

*When bananas are baked in their own skins, the flavor develops. Be sure, however, to have bananas that have slightly greenish tips. For additional flavor, use coconut-flavored rum instead of plain rum.*

6 large bananas, ripe, but with green tips
¼ cup firmly packed light brown sugar
½ cup coconut rum
1 cup sweetened flaked coconut, toasted

Preheat the oven to 400°F.

Place bananas, unpeeled, in a baking dish. Bake for 15 minutes. Remove skins and place on individual serving plates. Sprinkle evenly with brown sugar (about a tablespoon per banana). Warm the rum in a small pan, then ignite. Pour the flaming rum over the bananas. Shake pan until flames are extinguished. Sprinkle bananas with toasted coconut and serve immediately on individual serving plates.

Contrary to what you'd think, bananas are picked when they are green because they develop a better flavor when they ripen off the tree.

**Serves:** 6

# Honey Ambrosia

*This old-fashioned dessert goes together quickly, especially if you keep jarred orange and grapefruit sections in your refrigerator. When in season, strawberries and/or blueberries can replace any of the fruit.*

3 fresh oranges

3 fresh grapefruit

½ small fresh pineapple

¼ cup orange juice

¼ cup honey

½ cup sweetened flaked or shredded coconut

Peel and section the oranges and grapefruit. Peel and dice the pineapple and mix with the orange and grapefruit sections. Mix the orange juice and honey. Turn the fruit into a serving bowl or bowls and pour the honey mixture over. Sprinkle with the coconut.

According to Greek mythology, "ambrosia" is the food of the gods. It has come to mean a chilled fruit dessert, usually including coconut.

**Serves:** 4

# Mango Raisin Flambé

*Tropical fruits lend themselves beautifully to flambé. You can substitute fresh pineapple or banana chunks if you wish or include all three fruits if you triple the recipe.*

1 ounce (¼ stick) butter
¼ cup packed light or dark brown sugar
¼ cup slivered almonds
1 ripe mango, peeled, seeded, and cubed
½ cup golden or dark raisins
¼ cup dark rum
1 pint vanilla ice cream

Place a medium-sized skillet over moderate heat. Add the butter and brown sugar and cook until bubbly. Add the almonds and stir until they are toasted. Add the mango and raisins, reduce heat to low, and cook just until the mango is heated through and the raisins are plump. Pour the rum into a metal ladle or long-handled metal pan. Ignite rum and pour it over the fruit in the pan. Rotate the pan, stirring, until flames are extinguished.

Scoop ice cream into six dessert dishes and spoon the fruit and sauce over.

**Serves:** 6

# Strawberry and Rhubarb Tart

*When rhubarb and strawberries are in season, make this quick and delicious tart using frozen puff pastry.*

1 cup orange juice

1 tablespoon lemon juice

½ cup sugar

2 cups thinly sliced rhubarb stalks (¼-inch-thick slices)

1 pint (8 ounces) fresh strawberries, cleaned, stemmed, and halved

1 sheet frozen puff pastry (from a 17¼-ounce package), thawed

Sugar for dusting

Preheat the oven to 400°F. Place oven rack in the center position.

Stir the orange juice, lemon juice, and sugar together in a bowl. Add the sliced rhubarb and strawberries. Set aside.

Cut the pastry in half lengthwise and place on a lightly floured surface. With a floured rolling pin, roll each piece to make 11x7-inch rectangles. Arrange rectangles on an ungreased baking sheet. Fold edges of the rectangles upward to make a half-inch border around both rectangles. With a fork, poke holes all over the centers of the pastries. Strain the rhubarb and strawberries and reserve liquid. Top the pastry rectangles with rhubarb and strawberries, dividing equally between the two sheets of pastry. Bake for 30 minutes or until pastry is golden. While tarts bake, pour the reserved liquid into a small saucepan and heat to simmering; reduce to about ¼ cup. Transfer tarts to a cooling rack. Brush with the reserved glaze and sprinkle with sugar.

**Serves:** 8

# Sugar-Baked Pears with Minted Cream

*You don't even need to peel or core the pears in this simple recipe. Just bake the pears whole and serve with a dollop of mint-flavored whipped cream. This makes a simple and elegant holiday dessert. Surround the dessert bowl with pine boughs if you wish.*

6 small Seckel, Bartlett, Bosc, or Anjou pears

¼ cup granulated sugar

1 cup heavy whipping cream

¼ cup powdered sugar

2 tablespoons green crème de menthe

Preheat the oven to 375°F. Butter a 9x13-inch baking dish.

Scrub the pears, dry them, and cut a thin slice from the bottom of each so the pears will stand up. Stand the pears in the baking pan. Sprinkle with the granulated sugar. Bake for 45 minutes, or until the pears are just tender. Remove from the oven and cool.

Whip the cream, adding the powdered sugar and crème de menthe. Serve one pear per serving, with the cream on the side to spoon over individual servings.

The Seckel Pear is a small, slightly russet-colored pear that is better for poaching or baking than for eating out of hand. It is available late August through December. It's ideal for this recipe because of its size.

**Serves:** 6

# Tropical Fruits with Sour Cream Ginger Sauce

*Light and refreshing, this is a perfect dessert when tropical fruits are in season. The creamy ginger sauce is simple to stir up, too. For a pretty presentation when serving a crowd, offer the fruits on a platter and let guests select their favorites. Put the Sour Cream Ginger Sauce into a bowl and have guests spoon it onto their individual servings.*

1 large Mexican papaya, peeled, seeded, and sliced

1 ripe, fresh pineapple, peeled and eyes removed, thinly sliced

2 or 3 large oranges, peeled and sliced or sectioned

2 bananas, peeled and sliced

Fresh mint leaves

Sour Cream Ginger Sauce:

1 cup light sour cream

1½ tablespoons honey

1½ tablespoons finely chopped crystallized ginger

Arrange the prepared fruits either on individual plates or on one large platter. Garnish with fresh mint leaves.

For the sauce, stir the sour cream, honey, and ginger together. Turn into a serving bowl to spoon over individual servings of the fruit.

**Serves:** about 8

# You Need It Now? Treats

Last-minute, crowd-pleasing treats

- Chocolate Peanut Butter Sundaes

- Minted Chocolate Sundaes

- Easy Ice Cream

- Ricotta with Honey and Sunflower Nuts

- Chocolate Quesadillas

- Cinnamon Tortilla Crisps

- Cranberry Fruit Dip

- Fruit and Nut Cereal Bars

- Gingered Fresh Strawberries

- Grapes with Sour Cream

- Sugar Crispies

- Toffee Squares

- Tortilla Pear Tart

- Trail Mix Treats

# Chocolate Peanut Butter Sundaes

*Need a great dessert right now? Keep good ice cream in the freezer and stir up a peanut butter-maple syrup sauce. This goes well with any variety of chocolate ice cream as well as coffee ice cream. For extra crunch, top it off with toasted chopped peanuts.*

1 pint chocolate or coffee ice cream, or ½ pint of each flavor
½ cup real maple syrup
⅓ cup smooth or chunky peanut butter
Chopped toasted peanuts, if desired

Scoop ice cream into serving dishes. In a glass pitcher or bowl, combine the maple syrup with the peanut butter and stir. To make the sauce more pourable, microwave on high power for about 30 seconds. Pour or spoon the sauce over the individual scoops and top with the chopped peanuts, if using.

**Serves:** 4

# Minted Chocolate Sundaes

*Of course you could buy chocolate sundae sauce, but your own homemade mint chocolate topping, made by infusing fresh mint, is by far the best! For a double chocolate sundae, serve the sauce over chocolate ice cream.*

½ cup chopped fresh mint
½ cup unsweetened cocoa powder
½ cup sugar
1 cup heavy whipping cream
Vanilla ice cream

In a medium-sized saucepan, combine the mint, cocoa powder, sugar, and cream. Heat to simmering. Strain. Let cool to warm. The sauce thickens as it cools. Serve warm sauce over scoops of ice cream.

**Serves:** 4

# Easy Ice Cream

*This is a fun recipe to make with kids. You can use plain half-and-half, chocolate milk, or eggnog (during the holidays) to make this really simple ice cream. It's sort of a "boy scout" recipe, but when there are kids around it keeps them entertained — for a while! Have each kid make their own ice cream for a fun party activity.*

½ cup half-and-half, chocolate milk, or eggnog

½ teaspoon vanilla extract

1 tablespoon sugar

2 (quart-size) zipper-seal or zip-top plastic freezer bags

1 (gallon-size) zipper-seal or zip-top plastic freezer bag

4 cups crushed ice (or snow)

4 tablespoons salt

Mix the half-and-half, chocolate milk, or eggnog with the vanilla and sugar in one of the 1-quart bags. Be sure to squeeze out as much of the air as possible. Close and place bag into the second 1-quart bag, squeeze out the air, and seal the second bag.

Place the small bags inside the gallon-size bag and add the ice and salt. Press out all the air again. Wrap the bag in a towel and shake and massage the bag for 5 to 8 minutes. During this time, the milk mixture will freeze into ice cream. Remove fresh ice cream from the inside bag and serve.

**Serves:** 1

# Ricotta with Honey and Sunflower Nuts

*Select a flavorful honey for this super-simple, last-minute dessert.*

⅓ cup ricotta

1–2 tablespoons warmed honey

1 tablespoon toasted and salted sunflower nuts

Scoop the ricotta into a serving dish. Drizzle with the honey, and sprinkle with sunflower nuts. That's it!

**Serves:** 1

# Chocolate Quesadillas

*For a new twist on S'mores, try this recipe.*

6 flour tortillas

1 ounce (¼ stick) melted butter

3 (1.55-ounce) bars milk chocolate, unwrapped

12 marshmallows

Vanilla ice cream

Heat oven to 450°F. Brush both sides of each tortilla with melted butter; place in single layer on ungreased cookie sheet. Place half of a candy bar on half of each tortilla and top the chocolate with 2 marshmallows. Fold each tortilla in half to form half-moon shape. Bake for 4 to 6 minutes or until golden brown. Top each with a scoop of vanilla ice cream.

**Serves:** 6

# Cinnamon Tortilla Crisps

*Something a little sweet, a little crisp, may be just the answer to dessert in a minute. Keep flour tortillas on hand and you've got 99% of what you need for these irresistible treats.*

⅓ cup sugar
1½ teaspoons ground cinnamon
Vegetable oil
10 flour tortillas

Combine sugar and cinnamon in a small bowl. Pour vegetable oil into a frying pan to a depth of about ½ inch and place over medium-high heat. Add the flour tortillas, one at a time, and cook until golden and puffy, about 30 seconds on each side. Drain on paper towels. While still warm, sprinkle tortillas on one side with the cinnamon-sugar mixture.

If you'd rather, cut the tortillas into wedges before you fry them. Serve them in a napkin-lined basket. They go well with ice cream.

**Serves:** 10

# Cranberry Fruit Dip

*This is an almost instant dessert. Just mix three ingredients to make a dip for fresh fruit.*

1 cup heavy whipping cream
1 (3-ounce) package cream cheese, softened
1 cup whole-berry cranberry sauce
Strawberries, grapes, pineapple chunks, banana chunks, or kiwi fruit for dipping

Pour cream in a medium bowl and beat with a hand mixer until stiff peaks form. Beat in the cream cheese and cranberry sauce on medium speed until well blended. Turn into a serving bowl and surround with fresh fruit for dipping.

**Serves:** 12 to 16

# Fruit and Nut Cereal Bars

*Grab any combination of dry cereals you might have on hand to make these bars and mix them with any dried fruits, nuts, or seeds.*

4 cups dry breakfast cereal (corn flakes, bran flakes, oat cereal, etc.)

1 cup dried cranberries, raisins, dates, or dried fruit bits

½ cup roasted unsalted sunflower nuts or pumpkin seeds

½ cup dry-roasted peanuts or chopped walnuts or pecans

¾ cup packed brown sugar

½ cup corn syrup

¼ cup creamy peanut butter

1 teaspoon vanilla extract

Coat a 9-inch square pan with cooking spray.

In a large bowl, combine the cereal, dried fruit, and nuts.

In a small saucepan, stir the brown sugar, corn syrup, and peanut butter together. Place over medium-high heat, and stir until mixture comes to a boil. Remove from the heat and stir in the vanilla. Pour the syrup over the cereal, fruit, and nut mix. Toss to coat everything with the syrup. Firmly press mixture into the prepared pan. Cool and cut into bars.

**Makes:** 32 bars

# Gingered Fresh Strawberries

*After you've eaten your fill of fresh strawberries, consider this easy-to-make dessert. Arrange the fresh berries in a shallow casserole, and if need be, get them ready for broiling several hours in advance — just cover and refrigerate until you are ready to serve dessert. This is best served very warm!*

1 pint (2 cups) fresh strawberries
1 teaspoon crystallized ginger
¼ cup sour cream
¼ cup packed brown sugar
Ice cream for serving (optional)

Clean and halve the strawberries and arrange in a shallow 1½-quart baking dish. Chop the ginger into fine pieces and sprinkle over the berries. Spoon the sour cream over the top and sprinkle with brown sugar.

Immediately before serving, preheat the broiler. Broil the strawberries 4 to 6 inches from the heat for 3 to 4 minutes or until bubbly. Serve with ice cream, if desired.

**Serves:** 4

# Grapes with Sour Cream

*Here's a dessert that you can put together at the last minute, or make ahead and chill.*
*It is pretty if you use a combination of black, purple, and green seedless grapes.*

. . . . . . . . . . . . . . . . . . . . . . . . . . . . . . . . . . . . . . . . . . . . . . . . . . . . . . . . . . . . . . . . . . . . . . . . . . . . . . . . . . . . . . . . . . . . . . . . . .

2 pounds seedless grapes, washed and dried
1 cup sour cream
½ cup tightly packed light brown sugar
Grated orange zest

. . . . . . . . . . . . . . . . . . . . . . . . . . . . . . . . . . . . . . . . . . . . . . . . . . . . . . . . . . . . . . . . . . . . . . . . . . . . . . . . . . . . . . . . . . . . . . . . . .

In a large bowl, combine the grapes and sour cream just until grapes are coated. Scoop into eight individual serving dishes or spread out in a 1½-quart shallow serving dish. Sprinkle with the brown sugar and then with the orange zest.

**Serves:** 8

# Sugar Crispies

*Need a quick treat for a meeting? These are so easy to make and anyone who loves things that are sweet and crispy will love them. Keep a packet of won ton wrappers in the freezer so you can quickly make these treats. The wrappers are available in the refrigerated section of produce or Asian markets. These crispies are perfect served with ice cream or sherbet.*

12 won ton wrappers (from a 16-ounce package)
¼ cup sugar

Preheat the oven to 400°F.

Slice each won ton wrapper in half diagonally to make two triangles each. Place on a baking sheet, close together. Lightly brush each triangle with water and sprinkle each with sugar. Bake for 5 to 6 minutes until golden and crisp. Remove from the oven and cool.

**Makes:** 24

# Toffee Squares

*You just remembered that you promised treats for the 10:00 meeting. These toffee bars come together in a hurry if you have certain staples on hand.*

32 saltine crackers

8 ounces (2 sticks) butter

1 cup packed brown sugar

2 cups chocolate chips, semisweet or milk chocolate

1 cup chopped pecans, walnuts, or almonds

Preheat oven to 350°F. Coat a 15x10-inch baking sheet with nonstick spray.

Arrange the crackers on the pan close together to make a solid base for the bars.

In a saucepan, melt the butter and stir in the brown sugar until sugar is dissolved and looks like a caramel sauce. Pour this mixture over the crackers evenly.

Bake for 15 minutes. Remove from the oven and immediately sprinkle the chocolate chips evenly over the top. As the chips melt, spread the chocolate over the toffee mixture, then sprinkle with chopped nuts. (For nuttier-tasting nuts, toast the nuts while the caramel-topped crackers bake.)

Cool completely and break crackers apart carefully.

**Makes:** 32 squares

# Tortilla Pear Tart

*When you want a quick and easy snack or dessert, think of this, especially if you keep flour tortillas on hand for making quesadillas.*

. . . . . . . . . . . . . . . . . . . . . . . . . . . . . . . . . . . . . . . . . . . . . . . . . . . . . . . . . . . . . . . . . . . . . . . . . . . . . . . . . . . . . . . . . . .

1 ounce (2 tablespoons) butter

4 tablespoons sugar, divided

1 (10-inch) flour tortilla

1 large pear, peeled and sliced

4 tablespoons apricot jam

. . . . . . . . . . . . . . . . . . . . . . . . . . . . . . . . . . . . . . . . . . . . . . . . . . . . . . . . . . . . . . . . . . . . . . . . . . . . . . . . . . . . . . . . . . .

Preheat the oven to 400°F. Place a large, flat skillet over medium heat. Melt the butter on the surface of the skillet. Sprinkle with 2 tablespoons of the sugar. Dip the tortilla in the butter-sugar mixture. Place the tortilla on a nonstick baking sheet.

Top the tortilla with the sliced pear. Sprinkle with the remaining sugar. Place into the oven and bake for 10 minutes. Brush with the apricot jam and serve hot, cut into wedges.

**Serves:** 4

# Trail Mix Treats

*Use your own favorite trail mix for these quick-to-put-together treats. They keep well in an airtight container in a cool place.*

. . . . . . . . . . . . . . . . . . . . . . . . . . . . . . . . . . . . . . . . . . . . . . . . . . . . . . . . . . . . . . . . . . . . . . . . . . . . . . . . .

1 cup (6 ounces) semisweet chocolate chips
2 cups trail mix, your favorite kind

. . . . . . . . . . . . . . . . . . . . . . . . . . . . . . . . . . . . . . . . . . . . . . . . . . . . . . . . . . . . . . . . . . . . . . . . . . . . . . . . .

Put the chocolate chips into a heatproof glass bowl, if using the microwave to melt the chocolate. Or, put them into a metal bowl over hot water. If using the microwave, heat the chips, 30 seconds at a time, stirring after each 30 seconds until chocolate is melted. If melting in a double boiler, stir frequently until chips are completely melted.

Put the trail mix into a bowl. Add the melted chocolate and stir until all the ingredients are coated with chocolate. Cover a cookie sheet with waxed paper and drop spoonfuls of the mixture onto the waxed paper. Let stand in a cool place until treats are set.

**Makes:** 24

# INDEX

# Acknowledgments

Thanks to my husband, Dick, who, as a willing taster has taste-tested most of the recipes in this book. Thanks, also, to my many friends (whom I will not name for fear I will forget someone) who willingly took recipes home and offered their approval and advice.

As I have always maintained, nothing we do happens in a vacuum. I, maybe more than anyone, depend on the reaction (and approval) of my friends and acquaintances. Many of these desserts have been long-time favorites. Others are abbreviated versions of old-time favorites.

Thank you to Megan Hiller and the staff at Sellers Publishing for allowing me to be part of this series of cookbooks. Thanks, also, to Jane Dystel, my persistent agent who just knows there is another project out there.